EVANSTON
WYOMING

Also available by Dennis J Ottley

Remembering (Korea: 1950-1953)

IZZARD INK PUBLISHING COMPANY
PO Box 522251
Salt Lake City, Utah 84152
www.izzardink.com

LIBRARY OF CONGRESS CONTROL NUMBER: 2018960342

Designed by Alissa Rose Theodor
Cover Design by Andrea Ho
Cover Photograph by Shelly & Deann Horne of Creative Ink Images
Cover Images: Robert Castillo/Shutterstock.com ivangal/Shutterstock.com
monofaction/Shutterstock.com

First Edition January 28, 2019

Contact the author at djottleybooks@gmail.com

Hardback ISBN: 978-1-64228-011-1
Softback ISBN: 978-1-64228-015-9
eBook ISBN: 978-1-64228-016-6

1967 to 1995

EVANSTON
WYOMING

VOLUME ONE

BOOM-BUST-POLITICS
"IN THE EYES OF A MAYOR"

DENNIS J OTTLEY

IZZARD INK
—PUBLISHING—

I dedicate this book to my wife, SANDY; the most important person in my life, whom I have loved very much over the years.

An Ideal First Lady...
Sandy has been at my side for almost 68 years and over these years we have walked together hand in hand. She was the one person who inspired me to write this book, and encouraged me to continue at times when things looked so dismal; plus, she edited the book as I wrote each chapter, and she has been my utmost Critic.

Sandy took a big part in my success in achieving my goals as a city official and side by side we always worked together. She has always been at my side giving me the faith, the support, the confidence, and the hope when things looked so bleak.

She has always been a great conversationalist, a great motivator of people, and appreciated by everyone.

She has been my wife, my partner, my nurse, my inspiration and my love all these years, plus, most of all, she is the Mother of my four sons; Rand, Dave, Tib, and Cody, giving them each her daily love.

Signed: Dennis J Ottley, Author

I like to see a man proud of the place he lives. I like to see a man live so that the place will be proud of him.

—ABRAHAM LINCOLN

U. F R ⁚ ... 1864. Cin ... ... Cole Creek

Photostat Copy of Pen Sketch of
James A. Evans, Division Engineer, U.P.R.R.,
said to have been made in 1864 by
Percy Thorne Brown, Ass't Engineer, U.F.R.R.,

This sketch was located from the UPRR Archives in Omaha, NE and was the only picture of Evans that we know of in existence. The Town of Evanston was named after him.

The well-known photographer A.J. Russell photographed this
American-style locomotive at an unknown station in Wyoming in 1868.
Russell was hired by the Union Pacific to document the construction of
the railroad. (The antlers provide a nice Wyoming touch.)

INTRODUCTION

E VANSTON, WYOMING, established in 1868. A tent city, a Hell on Wheels, founded during the construction of the First Transcontinental Railroad, the Union Pacific Railroad, with an elevation of 6,749 feet. The railroad arrived in the area in November 1868, and by December the rails had reached Evanston and the first train arrived on December 16, 1868 and the town began to grow. The railroad track followed the old Mormon trail partway through Uinta County.

Harvey Booth, named as Evanston's first businessman, opened up a saloon/restaurant in a tent near what is now Front Street. Later, when Mr. Booth was sheriff, he was found murdered in his livery stable located on the corner of what is now 10th Street and Center. His killer was never found, making this crime the oldest unsolved murder case in Uinta County and possibly in the state of Wyoming.

Evanston was named after James A. Evans, a young Union Pacific Railroad division surveyor, who surveyed the eastern half of the U.P. Line through what is now Wyoming. U.P. Chief Engineer Grenville Dodge, in 1869, surveyed the first platted subdivision in Evanston, titled the "Original Town of Evanston". At that time Mr. Dodge named the town in honor of Young James Evans, and on September 6, 1870 the Town of Evanston became the County Seat of Uinta County

The first plat included the southwesterly side of what is now Front Street up to the northeasterly side of what is now Summit Street, and the southeasterly side of 1st Street (presently 6th Street) to the northwesterly side of 10th Street (presently 15th Street).

Like other railroad towns through Wyoming, Chief Engineer Dodge platted the original town parallel to the railroad tracks, with the tracks going through town, causing the town to lay somewhat off compass. North Evanston, located across the tracks off China Mary Road in the area of 1st and 2nd Avenues and A, B, C and D Avenues, was also later platted parallel to the tracks. That area of North Evanston was called the "Union Pacific Subdivision."

Dr. Francis H. Harrison bought the first platted lot of the Original Town of Evanston for $200.00 and built his home. It was, and still is, located on the corner of 9th Street and Center Street across from the Uinta County Court House. The building is still in use as the office of the Evanston Business Leadership Network.

Later, in 1871, a machine shop and roundhouse were constructed, giving Evanston the longevity that many other railroad towns never received, and later a train depot was built. Early in the 20th Century a newer and much larger machine shop and roundhouse were built. They were both constructed of brick and large enough to handle the newer and larger locomotives. The new roundhouse was a half circle structure with an outside turntable, with tracks running into each section of the roundhouse from the turntable, which is still in existence.

In 1873 Evanston was incorporated as an official town and a Mr. Brown was elected mayor. It has been said that Evanston was the first officially incorporated community in the Territory of Wyoming. However, on account of lack of finances the town went broke and lost its incorporated status two years later. Then, on June 23, 1888, Evanston was once again incorporated and Dr. Francis H. Harrison was elected as mayor, with Harvey Booth, D. D. Marx, John Brew and Frank M. Foote as Council members. A town government was once again established. Dr. Harrison, whom the present 11th Street (Harrison Drive) was later named for, was elected mayor and held the office until 1890, at which time I. C. Winslow was elected mayor for the next two terms (total of four Years).

One thing in favor of Evanston was the Bear River running through it. With the abundance of timber relatively nearby, the waterway of the Bear made Evanston a refueling stop for cross-country locomotives. Coal was mined a few miles north of Evanston in an area that they call Almy. Evanston had a large population of Chinese workers that the railroad transported to the area to work on the railroad. They lived on the north side of the railroad tracks in a small "Chinatown". Located in this small Chinese community was one of only three Chinese Joss Houses (Chinese Houses of Worship) in the United States, built in 1874. The other two were in San Francisco, California and New York City, New York.

As a Wyoming Statehood Centennial project, in 1990 the community, under the leadership of the very dedicated and hardworking citizen Ann Bell, had a replica of the original Joss House constructed, which is presently located on Front Street in what they now call Depot Square.

Dr. Francis H. Harrison
Mayor
1888-1889   1897-1899

Evanston's first Mayor following the second and final time of incorporation as an official town.

1st Council's Minutes

On this date, 100 years ago, the first city council meeting of the re-organized government of Evanston was held. Here is a copy of the minutes of that first meeting. The original minutes were handwritten.

Record of the Town Council

of the

Town of Evanston

Uinta County Wyoming Territory

June 23d A.D. 1888

And now on this 23d day of June A.D. 1888 the following named gentlemen having been duly notified by the Certificate of the County Clerk of Uinta County Wyoming Territory of their election to the respective offices in the Town of Evanston and for said Town and having duly qualified as required by law appeared in session as the Council of said Town as follows to wit!

F.H. Harrison	*Mayor*
O.D. Marx	*Councilman*
John Brew	*"*
Harvey Booth	*"*
F.M. Foote	*"*

Thereupon in compliance with Section 459 of the Revised Statutes of Wyoming Territory it was decided by lot that of the Councilmen above named O.D. Marx and John Brew should hold such office for the term of two years and that Harvey Booth and F.M. Foote should hold such office for the term of one year as provided by law.

Order for Books Blanks and Stationary was given John Morris Company. and Petitions for the offices of Marshal and Deputy Marshal of said Town were presented and read and action thereon deferred to some subsequent meeting and on motion agreed to by all said Council adjourned until Tuesday June 26th A.D. 1888 at 8 P.M.

Signed

Mayor

The coal mines at Almy were deep mines. After the railroad was completed many of the Chinese workers went to work at the mines. Working at these mines proved to be very dangerous. There were two separate explosions that killed hundreds of the miners, both local citizens and Chinese. These mines were deep underground, with gas pockets making them so dangerous that the Union Pacific Railroad (U.P.R.R.) decided to shut them down in the 1920s. After that the Chinese population dwindled, disappearing almost completely in the 1930s. This left two well-known and respected Chinese people who lived and died here. They were known as Mormon Charlie and China Mary, both a large part of Evanston's history.

It is also known that Chief Washakie of the Shoshoni tribe camped west of Evanston in the vicinity of the current Dunmar Best Western Motel. The tribe camped there back during the summer, and came to town often to trade and barter with the local merchants.

Evanston later became a major tourist stop on the Lincoln Highway (U.S. Highway 30 S). The highway ran east and west through Wyoming, creating a primary tourist stop for highway traffic in Evanston. The Lincoln Highway was one of the few major highways running coast to coast in the United States.

Evanston was, at the time, well known for the gambling and prostitution that apparently was legal in Wyoming and very active along the Lincoln Highway and the U.P.R.R. Every saloon, bar and liquor store in town had card tables, roulette tables, crap (dice) tables and slot machines in their establishments, and in addition, every hotel/motel, restaurant and service station had slot machines. They even had gambling on the passenger trains as they entered Wyoming, though it was illegal as soon as they left the state on both ends. Prostitution was housed in different locations on Front Street, but in the late 1940s there was only one brothel left, called the Palace Rooms. At that time it was located upstairs above a café called the Rail Café.

There were many reports and claims of corruption and illegal acts going on throughout southern Wyoming during the time of gambling and prostitution. Consequently, in 1951, gambling and prostitution became illegal in Wyoming. This caused a lot of concern for some of the business people and local officials. They worried that the town would lose an enormous amount of its tourist business, and that would cause the town to lose an excessive amount of revenue.

Evanston is a typical Wyoming community surrounded by cattle and sheep ranches, but it has gone through many changes. At times some believed it might even become deserted and maybe just another ghost town, but it has been a community of strong-minded folks that refused to believe that. Some called Evanston a bedroom community to Salt Lake City and the Wasatch Front in Utah, but in all reality, Evanston is and has always been its own community. It has been a community of survival. It has gone through a lot of hard times, but has always come through. It has also seen a lot of good times. It is and has always been a community of proud and hard-working folks as this story will point out.

"In every community, there is work to be done.
In every nation, there are wounds to heal.
In every heart, there is power to do it."

— QUOTE BY MARIANNE WILLIAMSON

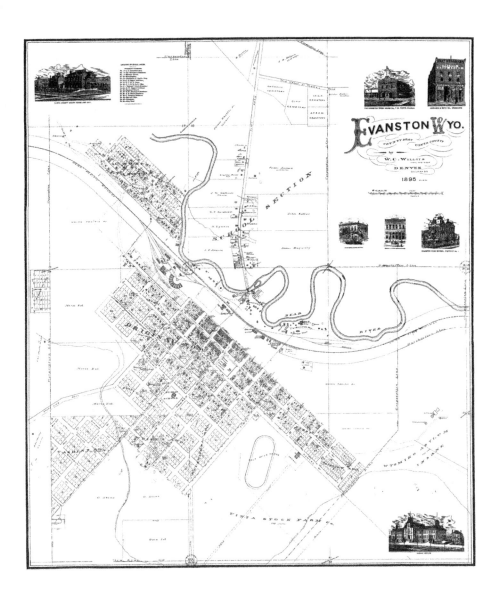

Main Street ~ Evanston Wyoming 1906

Evanston, Wyoming in past history has also been known as *"The Queen City of the Rockies."* This community grew from a railroad tent city in 1868 to a community of over 12,000 citizens in today's count.

PART ONE

" CITY COUNCILMAN "

Ben Stein once said, *"It all will come your way, once you understand that you have to make it come your way, by your own exertions."*

CHAPTER ONE

The beginning....It was the end of May of 1952, I had just returned home from Korea after serving almost two years of active duty in the United States Army, about half of that time as a tank commander in Korea. It was great to be home again, to be with my wife Sandy and my son Randy, who was about to have his first birthday on June 3, 1952. Sandy's 19th birthday would be the day after, on June 4th. Luckily, I had got home just in time for both of them. I had turned 20 years old that year on January 28th.

When I came home it didn't seem like the town had changed much, except maybe it was a little quieter. Probably because of the absence of gambling now that the state had made it illegal in 1951. When I left Evanston in 1950, gambling and prostitution was wide open in Wyoming, especially along the U.S. Highway 30 corridor. When I got home I found there were no longer slot machines anywhere in sight, the bars had gotten rid of all their gambling tables and the Palace Rooms (the house of prostitution) had been shut down. It seemed to make a big difference in the town.

Nevertheless, it felt great to be home, maybe a little strange after being in the army and spending the past year in Korea. I had no idea what to expect. I thought to myself, *I hope I don't have any problems* or *difficulty adjusting to being a husband again and now a father*, then I started wondering about being able to find a job. I had no idea where to even start looking, but I got lucky. The folks that owned the East End Texaco Service, where I worked before I went into the service, came to me and offered me my old job back. When I had left, the place was owned by Bill and Delores Kitchens, but while I was in Korea they had sold it to a couple of brothers, Preston and Fay Eyre. They were great to work for, and I really appreciated them for giving me the job. It was a big worry off my mind.

Within two days after arriving home I was now back working my old job. It didn't pay all that much, but it was a job, and I was damn thankful for it. Plus, with Sandy waiting tables at the Ranch Café, we were able to make enough between us to survive and make ends meet.

The only extra pay I got from being in the service and serving overseas was what they called "mustering-out pay". It amounted to $300.00. Getting that money helped a lot at the time. It helped us in buying an old used Packard from Miles Alexander's used car lot at a fair and affordable price. I don't recall the year or how much we paid for it, but it was something we could afford at the time.

After being discharged and coming home, I think we were all quite surprised and kind of disappointed by the "welcome back" we got from the folks. You would have thought that there would have been some kind of a greeting from the town people, other than just our families, maybe a handshake or something welcoming us home, but folks acted like we had never been gone. No questions about how we liked the service or of our experiences and our time in Korea, nothing about how the war was going or anything. They treated us as if we had never left, but that was okay. Actually, you wouldn't have even thought there was a war going on. Even if they had asked about it, they probably wouldn't have known where Korea was anyway. Most of us didn't give it much thought. There weren't too many of us that wanted to talk about it anyway. We were more concerned with getting back to living a normal life again and getting a job.

My brother, Kent, had been discharged from the army a few months before I was and got a job as a locomotive fireman on the Union Pacific Railroad early that spring. His father-in-law was a locomotive engineer (known as a hoghead) on the U.P.R.R. at the time, and he talked Kent into hiring out. It was a good high-paying job, but it would probably be several years before he would be able to work the whole year round. The first several years he would probably only work three to six months out of twelve, but in time it would end up being a good year-round job.

In the spring of 1953, Kent told me that they were starting to hire locomotive firemen again on the railroad and told me I should put my name in, so I applied and got hired. I felt pretty bad quitting Eyre Brothers, because they were great to work for, but I would be making 2 to 3 times the money working on the railroad. They understood and were great about it.

On June 5, 1953, the day after Sandy's birthday, she gave birth to our second son, David. I was glad now that I changed to a job that paid better, because we now had an addition to the family and a hospital bill that needed to be paid. With the new job we would be able to afford a little more.

When I started work as a railroad fireman, I had to make several student runs with experienced firemen before I would be on my own. We had to learn to fire and service all different types of steam engines, diesel units and the "GE Big Blow". It took me about seven student trips before they finally signed me off as being qualified to go on my own. That particular year I was fortunate enough to work until October, which was longer than most people got in their first years when just starting out.

After getting laid off by the railroad that year, Kent and I both applied for a job with an oil field company called the Stove Creek Oil Company. Kent worked there for a short time, then he got a job at the Wyoming State Hospital as an aide, but I stayed with Stove Creek through that winter, and believe me, it was cold.

The oil company drilling site was located about 20 miles south of Evanston near the railroad tunnels. We were working on a large oil derrick using oil-based mud, because it was too cold to use water-based – it would freeze! When running pipe or anything else through mud, you would get so dirty from that oil-based mud that it could cause rashes on your legs, but I didn't mind: it was a job. It paid $400.00 per month, which wasn't too bad for the times. The worst part was working night shifts, but we traded off, giving us a chance to work days sometimes. They did furnish us with one meal during the shift and sometimes gasoline for our vehicles.

I worked as a roughneck on the floor for a couple of months and then I got promoted to work the monkey board – that's what they called the derrick at the top. I worked up there as monkey man until

I hurt my back while helping out on the floor. My back was hurting so bad that I had to spend several days in the hospital in traction. I was out of work for almost a month because of it, but the company still paid me my regular wage, holding nothing out except taxes.

My mother died in April of 1954 while I was still working for Stove Creek. They gave me a few days off with pay for the funeral and to be with my family for a while, which I really appreciated. They were a good company to work for, other than it being so the cold during the winter months, but I did enjoy the work and liked the guys I worked with. The work was very interesting and I learned a lot, but I was now waiting for the railroad to call me back to work as a fireman.

It wasn't until June when the railroad finally called me back. I fired on the engines throughout that summer, but it ended up being a shorter work year than 1953 was. When September came I was laid off again. I was kind of disappointed because I was hoping to work at least until October.

All during that winter of 1954 and 1955 I worked three jobs, sometimes all during the same period but at different hours. I was hired on at the railroad freight house and depot as a waybill clerk and a janitor. My work hours varied depending on what we were scheduled to work on: checking the railway cars in the yard or cleaning the depot and freight house. I also worked part time at the Evanston Cash (IGA) Grocery Store for Ed Wheeler, stacking shelves and cleaning up. My third job was working at Al's Frontier Truck Stop, owned by Albert Hutchings. It was open 24 hours a day, so I worked there a lot during the graveyard shift, servicing trucks, and other vehicles.

We mostly serviced trucks, repairing their tires or putting on chains if they were going east in the winter time. The eastbound trucks always had to have chains on to get over a cluster of three hills called "The Three Sisters"—so named because they were close together, and were long and very steep going both ways. They could be damn treacherous in the winter time, especially when it stormed.

A good part of the time we would have to meet the truck on the road to the truck to put chains on, or even help thaw the truck out if it was frozen—diesel fuel has a tendency to freeze up when truck is running in severe cold and stormy weather. We used a lot of a product called Heat, which we added to their fuel to get the engine unthawed. Sometimes we used as much as a case of Heat to get the job done. We also provided road service, to go out and change flat tires. It was icy cold at times out there on the road. We didn't have a large workshop where a truck could drive in to have its tire repaired or have other work done, so we had to do most of the work outside.

Albert Hutchings was a brother to my brother-in-law, Johnny, my sister's husband. Al had just purchased the truck stop from the Porter Brothers, Kilburn and Wayne. The Porters had actually only subleased the property from their Frontier oil distributor, Otto Kennedy, but they still owned the business.

The truck stop was owned by Frontier Refining Company who gave the first lease to Kennedy and his father, Reay. They were the distributors and jobbers and had a Frontier service station located where Dave's Custom Meat Shop is presently located, on the corner of County Road and Bear River Drive.

Otto Kennedy got the Frontier Refining Company to build the truck stop on the west end. After building it in 1951, Frontier leased it to the Kennedys. The Kennedys subsequently subleased it to the Porters, who in 1954 sold their lease to Al Hutchings.

I worked for Al for the rest of that winter. He had been a cook in cafés most of his adult life and had never operated anything like a service station or a truck stop, and he thought he might need someone with some experience. So, as I had a lot of experience in servicing trucks and repairing their tires, he wanted me to stay on and help him. The other jobs I had that winter were temporary and didn't last long.

One of my best friends from my high school in Vernal, Utah was Paul Oaks. Paul was killed In North Korea on November 9, 1950 during the Korean War, but his body for burial was not sent home until January, 1955. His mother had called me to be a pallbearer at his funeral, and I accepted. Sandy and I and our two sons, Rand and Dave, went to his funeral. When we got back to Evanston I continued to work for Al at the truck stop. I believe he was paying me about ninety cents per hour, and I stayed with him the rest of that winter.

That June of 1955, when the railroad called me back to work as a fireman, Al Hutchings offered me the opportunity to buy 50% of his ownership in the business and become half owner. It was really a tough decision. I discussed it with Sandy, but she just told me it was up to me.

Working for the railroad, I was getting laid off every fall for a time—I had no way of knowing how long—but I knew that once I got to the point of working year round, it would be a great job. Still, I had always wanted to go into my own business and Al was giving me that opportunity. So I chose to stay at the truck stop and give up my seniority with the railroad. It was possible I had made a mistake, I thought, but only time would tell. On March 29, 1957 Sandy gave birth to our third son Tib, named after his Grandpa Fotheringham, Sandy's dad. We now had three sons and felt like we needed more room than we had while renting.

At this time, my brother Kent was building a new home up on the hill in west Evanston, and he offered to sell his house on 1st Avenue in North Evanston to us for $3,500.00. We went to the bank and borrowed the money to buy it and moved our family to North Evanston. We lived there the next three years.

In 1957, after Al Hutchings and I had been partners for two years, he decided to sell out and go back to Oklahoma, where he was originally from. Unfortunately, I didn't have the money to buy him out at that time, so he sold his half interest to our gasoline jobber and distributor, Otto Kennedy; his father, Reay; and Otto's brother-in-law, Ralph Calvert. However, I would still be half owner and the manager of the operation.

At this time Bob, my younger brother, had just been discharged from the Air Force and had started working for the truck stop. To keep him on board, I offered to sell ten percent of the ownership to him, leaving me owning only forty percent. I would still be the manager of the operation, but I got along well with both Ralph and Bob, who would be partners in the business. They worked right with me in taking good care of the place, and both showed a lot of interest. I felt that someday Bob and I might have the opportunity to buy the rest of the partners out and have complete ownership of the business. The oil company actually owned the property; we only owned the business, but we did have a good sub-lease with the Kennedys.

In August of 1960 we used my G.I. loan to build a new home in west Evanston near where Kent built. It was a nice home with a lot more room than what we had been used to. Sandy loved it. We lived there for the next 31 years!

On October 27, 1964 Sandy gave birth to a fourth son. Sandy had a pretty tough time with him. He was premature and only weighed 4 pounds. We named him Cody. He was our last son. We now had four boys.

It was in the early 1970s when our distributor, Otto Kennedy, decided to let Bob and me buy his stock in the business. Since his father Reay had previously passed away, and his brother-in-law had left the business and moved to Kemmerer, Otto ended up buying them out and now had a 50% ownership. The business's name was Evanston Truck Terminal, Inc. We had incorporated the business when Al Hutchings left, but now Bob and I had full ownership of the corporation after buying Otto out. However, Otto remained our jobber and distributor. He was a great guy and one of the most honest people that I had ever been involved with.

During all these years I was getting involved heavily with community activities. My wife and I first started getting involved with Cub Scouts, her as a den mother and me as a committee member. Then I started a boxing club with the help of Chief of Police, John Martin, and my former boxing promoter, Lyman Brown, who had been a professional wrestler at one time. The boxing club helped a lot of kids, particularly some kids that were prone to getting into trouble. Chief Martin allowed me to set up a small gym in the basement of the old town hall where we built a mat and put up a couple of striking bags. It turned out to be a pretty good little gym where the kids could hang out and do a little training.

We had dozens of kids from all walks of life come down and try out our gym. Some came to learn how to box while others just came to do a little tumbling and hitting the bags, but most of those that stayed with it did a lot of boxing (sparring) and actually boxed in the ring when we had ring bouts. We took the boxers to different towns in Wyoming and Utah to compete in boxing contests. We even took several kids to the State of Wyoming Golden Gloves Tournament in Casper for years. One of them, Danny Hunter, took the Golden Gloves State Championship two years in a row, and one year Bruce Tueller came close to winning the state championship, but lost by a split decision in the end.

In 1962 Shelby Dill, Manager of the Chamber of Commerce, Kilburn Porter, a very active local businessman, and I started the Little League football program under Pop Warner rules. With some help, I kept that going for thirteen years, before Rick Sather and Marvin Munoz took over from me, and they kept it going until the recreation department decided it should be included in their program in 1976.

I was on the board of directors of the Evanston Chamber of Commerce for years, and I was elected president of the Evanston Cowboy Days Committee in 1963. At this time the committee had a pretty large deficit. We knew we had to do something to bring the committee out of debt. We hired Swanny Kirby's Bar T outfit as our stock producer, hoping Swanny would do a good job for us during the rodeo. He asked us what we wanted for a specialty act and we told him that we would like to bring in the famous "Ben Hur" act, both days if possible. He thought about it for a few minutes and said when he goes to the stock show in Denver, Colorado he would check into it.

He called me from Denver and told me he could book the act, but only for Monday, Labor Day, and it would cost $1,000.00. At that time we had the rodeo scheduled for Sunday and Monday only. I told him that I would canvass the committee and then call him back. The committee decided that we would like to have the act, even just for the one day. I told Swanny that the committee thought it would bring in enough money that day alone to pay for it. It did and then some.

We had three beautiful young ladies as Cowboy Days Royalty. MarJean Anderson was named Miss Cowboy Days, the queen of the rodeo. In previous years they would have called her "Cowboy Days Queen." We felt it was more proper to name her "Miss Cowboy Days," and we applied that to her banner. Her 1st Attendant was Linda Bowns from Almy, and her 2nd Attendant was Linda Eastman from Bridger Valley. All three were experienced horsewomen and had outstanding personalities, representing Evanston very well throughout the season.

Bob Burns was the chairman who oversaw the Royalty and with his wife, Connie and my wife, Sandy we took the girls to a professional seamstress, Mrs. Malouf, in Evanston and had the girls fitted with hand-sewn blue and red pantsuits with jackets. Mrs. Malouf and her husband, Mike, owned a ranch west of Evanston. The blue suit was for "Miss Cowboy Days" and the red suits were for the two attendants.

Swanny Kirby loaned Sandy and me a couple of horses to ride around town to promote Cowboy Days. Sandy had an Appaloosa and, as I recall, I had a roan. We went all over town on those horses trying to advertise the rodeos. We stopped a lot of tourists who were going through town, trying to get them to stay and attend the rodeos. This was on Saturday, and the first rodeo wouldn't be until the next day, Sunday. When we got back to the rodeo grounds with the horses late that afternoon, Swanny had told Sandy that she had been riding one of his bucking broncs, and sure enough, the next day that same Appaloosa came out of the shoots with a bronc rider on it. Sandy about fell over.

The committee also had a big "OK Corral shootout" that Saturday evening in front of the U.P. Depot using blank bullets. There was a large crowd watching the show and everyone seemed to enjoy it, especially when Brent Davis pretended to get shot and put on an act that got the crowd laughing so hard the rest of us couldn't help laughing also.

To the best of my knowledge 1963 was the first time that the American flag had been raised along with the Wyoming flag during the opening of the Cowboy Days rodeo event. In the past, the Nation's flag had been presented only during the grand entry on horseback. When the committee noticed that there was no flagpole at the arena, it was decided that not only should there be a flagpole, but that the Star Spangled Banner should be raised along with the State of Wyoming's flag at the opening of each event.

When it was brought up in a meeting, the idea was that maybe the committee could get hold of one of those 70-foot-high TV antennas that had been removed from people's yards because now TV antennas were installed on roofs and didn't need to be so high. It was mentioned that Cazin and Houtz had been taking those high towers down for people and that they had a stockpile of them. It was suggested that I approach Cazin and Houtz about purchasing one of those poles and if they would be interested in putting it up at the rodeo arena.

When we went to talk to Jerry Cazin about it and explained what we had in mind, he said that if this was for the committee and the rodeo, they would not only furnish the pole, but they would also put it up, plus set up the rope and pulleys so we could raise and lower the flags. In other words, he said, they would have it up and ready for use on the first day of the rodeo, and they did. There was no charge whatsoever. We couldn't believe it, but it sure was appreciated. We could now have a flag-raising and have someone singing the National Anthem prior to each event. That same flagpole is still being used at Cowboy Days rodeos. If I remember right, the first group to raise the flag was a Boy Scout group.

Jerry Cazin and Max Houtz were the owners of Cazin and Houtz, and they had helped the community in many various ways, especially in supporting the fire department. After Mr. Houtz passed away, Mr. Cazin purchased the store and changed the name to just Cazin's. They are still in business, operated by Cazin's three sons. It's probably the oldest local owned business in Evanston, and has been one of Evanston's finest.

In 1963, all bucking chutes and roping chutes were located at the east end of the arena facing west. There were five bucking chutes and that particular year the committee painted the numbers 1, 2, 3, 4 and 5 large enough to cover each entire gate. We did not have sponsors back in those days. The committee also had the south side bleachers painted. Everything that had to be repaired or painted at the rodeo arena had to be done by the Cowboy Days Committee. The Fair Board did nothing, but they still charged the committee 10% of the gate receipts.

The Sunday rodeo that Labor Day weekend turned out to have a relatively good crowd, but because of the "Ben Hur" act on Labor Day, on Monday we filled up the stadium so there wasn't even any standing room left. That year we brought the committee completely out of debt and had funds left over to start the next year.

Bob Burns was elected president of the committee for 1964. I remained on the committee for several years after that. I had a great committee to work with during 1963, and I hoped Bob would also have a good one.

I was elected president of the Evanston Junior Chamber of Commerce, better known as the Evanston Jaycees, for 1966-1967. That year the Evanston Jaycees took first place as number one chapter in the state of Wyoming, and I was honored as the outstanding local president of the state, plus we received and were honored with many, many other awards for outstanding service.

I had a terrific membership and a great board of directors with Clyde Wilson as past president and Chairman of the Board, John Proffit as First Vice President; Bob Schuetz as Second Vice-President, Dave Madia as Secretary, Marlin Wright as Treasurer, Myron Bell and Lee Taylor as Directors, and others such as Bob and Jack Mathson, Norman Garley, Gene Bell, Cloey Wall, Jesse Whiteman, Dee Orr Kunz, and my two brothers, Mack and Bob, plus many others that worked hard to earn all the honors. They all took a big part in making the Evanston Jaycees the number one chapter in the state in 1967.

At that time, the Jaycees was a young man's organization for men between the ages of 21 through 36. It stressed leadership, encouraged public speaking and training through community development participation. It was an honor to be a member at the time.

Sandy was president of the Evanston Jaycee Anns, at that same time. The Jaycee Anns was the auxiliary to the Evanston Jaycees.

She had a great membership that helped tremendously in making the Evanston chapter number one. The next year she became president of the Wyoming Jayceettes, the women's state auxiliary to the State of Wyoming Jaycees, and I became one of the state's National Directors, representing the state at the National meetings.

I was also Commander of the American Legion, Post 41 for two years from 1961 to 1963 during this period, and became a life member of the Veterans of Foreign Wars (V.F.W.). Both Sandy and I were very active in the community about this time. I was getting to appreciate our town more and more. The more I got involved, the more I became concerned with the community. I wanted Evanston to remain the good, clean, prosperous community it had been in the past, thanks to the Union Pacific Railroad.

In 1966, which was an election year, the Jaycee membership thought it would be advantageous to the Jaycees to have representation on the Evanston City Council. Roger Fife and I said we would run: Roger would be from Ward 3 and I would be from Ward 1. We both won and became members of the Evanston City Council. And that was the beginning of my political life.

CHAPTER 2

1967....The State of Wyoming set the date of filing for election on May 17, 1966. Both Roger Fife and I filed for city council and Bob Burns filed for mayor. There was no incumbent filing for Ward 1 or Ward 3, but James G. (Jim) Smith was an incumbent from Ward 2 and he was running for reelection. Fife and I both had opposition. Fife was opposed by Clarence Bateman and I was opposed by Richard R. Bouck. The incumbent mayor, Harold (Shorty) Raybourn was running for reelection against Bob Burns.

Previously, when Evanston was a town with a population of only about 3,500, the mayor and council were required to publicly designate their party affiliation; Democrat, Republican or whatever. Town politics at that time were partisan politics and were only for two-year terms.

In the early 1960s, during the time Shorty Raybourn was mayor, the Wyoming State Hospital was annexed to the Town of Evanston. This gave the Town of Evanston enough of an increase in population, approximately 4,000, to declare the community a First Class City, and was no longer considered just a town. The mayor and city council took the necessary action to make this happen.

The designation First Class City changed the politics to become nonpartisan and changed the terms of office to four years for both mayor and council members. Therefore, when we ran for election we were not required to declare our party affiliation. This was good as far as I was concerned, because it kept most of the politics out of city government. It should have kept all politics out, but I guess there is some politics in everything.

On November 8, 1966, the date of the election, Bob Burns was elected mayor. Fife, Smith and I were all elected as members of the city council, but would not be sworn in until the first meeting in January of 1967. At that time we would join the three other sitting council members. These were Arnold Christensen, Melvin Baldwin and William (Bill) George. Mayor Burns's first order of business was to make his official appointments. J. P. Hudson was re-appointed as City Clerk/Treasurer, Vincent Vehar as City Attorney, Joseph I. Williams as City Judge, Charles (Chuck) Overy as Chief of Police; and Ed Jones as Fire Chief. At that time the Evanston Fire Department was 100% volunteer. They were well trained and did a great job.

Our city council room was in the Old Town Hall building and not much larger than a normal size living room, no more than 200 square feet at the most. The council sat around an oblong shaped dining room table with the mayor in the middle facing the department heads and any visitors we may have had at the meeting. If we had much more than a dozen people visiting we would be crowded.

This made it bad for those that didn't smoke, because at that time smoking was permitted inside of buildings, and we made ash trays available for those who smoked. At the time Mayor Burns smoked either a pipe or a cigar. I and a couple other council members smoked, but I finally quit in September of 1969. Some of the visitors also smoked. I'm sure this caused the small meeting room to become quite uncomfortable for the non-smokers, but I don't recall anyone complaining.

In the next several months we discussed the possibility of building a curved bench where the mayor could sit in the middle, with three councilmen on each side of him looking slightly down to the people present. It would be better for us, we decided, to be facing the staff and other visitors. Councilman Arnold Christensen, who had done a lot of carpenter work, volunteered to get the bench built.

After all of the newly elected members were sworn in by the City Clerk, J. P. (Percy) Hudson, we all took our seats. Percy was also the City Treasurer. I was lucky: I got to sit on the side of the table facing the visitors. The city's regular meetings were only once a month at that time. The mayor was paid $100.00 a month and the council members were paid $10.00 per meeting. I got a check for

$10.00 each month except on the rare occasions that we happened to have a special meeting

The city's budget was set on a fiscal year, July 1st through June 30th. The 1966-1967 budget was about $310,000.00; approximately $235,000.00 for the general fund and $75,000.00 for the water fund. The water fund was what they called an enterprise fund. Moneys collected from water use had to be used for that only. This was a state law.

The Wyoming sales tax was only 3% at the time and Evanston was only receiving from the Wyoming Department of Revenue about $48,000.00 to $50,000.00 a year from sales and use tax. Other funds were from the 8 mill levy collected through Uinta County for property tax and some from the state mineral taxes. It was not much of a budget, even for those times.

The City was having some pretty tough times. They seriously needed to upgrade the disposal plant located by the Bear River at the far end of Sims Lane just off First Avenue. The plant was over 25 years old and was much too small to handle the increased sewage flow. It had recently been improved with upgraded machinery and equipment, but it still couldn't handle the capacity of the present flow. Both the Wyoming and Utah State Health Departments were concerned over the pollution of the Bear River.

During the July meeting of that year Mayor Bob Burns and the city council voted unanimously to call for a special election and appeal to the citizens of Evanston to vote Yes on a proposal in an upcoming election scheduled for July 11th to authorize the issuance of $200,000.00 in municipal bonds to construct a new sewage disposal plant to replace the present one, which was inoperative and outdated.

One of the Evanston Jaycees' major projects was what they called the "Get Out to Vote Campaign." Through this program the Jaycees tried to encourage everyone to go to the polls and vote. They advertised that if there was any one person(s) that couldn't get to the polls and needed a ride or assistance, they could call a certain telephone number and one of the members of the Jaycees would go see that they got their opportunity to vote. The Jaycees kept this program going during every election for many years. One stipulation was that a member could, under no circumstances, discuss with a voter anything about what was on the ballot or who to vote for. If the voter asked a member to explain what an amendment or something of that sort the member could explain it to them, but could not tell them how to vote. The member would just tell them to use their own judgment. The Uinta County Herald issue on July 6, 1967 had the headline, SEWER BOND ELECTION JULY 11th. The voters turned out overwhelmingly in favor of the bond issue, giving the city enough funding to build on and upgrade the existing disposal plant. However, the engineering hadn't been completed yet, and bids weren't called for until sometime in May of 1968 and awarded the following June. Construction didn't start until August of 1968. It was to be at the same location and would be more than adequate for the present population. This made both the Utah and Wyoming Health Departments happy.

Included with the $200,000.00 bond issue that was passed we also got a grant for $45,000.00 from the Federal Water Pollution Control Administration. The engineers cost estimate for the sewer plant and lift station were approximately $180,000.00 plus the cost of some additional equipment.

There were other concerns that needed to be looked at, such as extensions of new water and sewer lines to new areas that had recently been annexed. Evanston's municipal airport needed work done on the runway, and the streets needed some improvements. During that time a good portion of Evanston streets were unimproved, and during the spring thaw they could get damn muddy, but money was so tight some things had to wait until funding was available. In some cases state and federal funds were available for certain programs, but we had to apply for them and then it was a matter of whether or not the applications got approval.

The State of Wyoming passed a new law concerning opening hours for liquor licensed establishments, so the towns and cities both had to amend their present ordinance to coincide with the new state law. Soon after the state had passed the new law the Evanston liquor dealers immediately approached the city to act on the law. This was one of the first ordinances that the council acted on in 1967 and probably the most controversial.

On May 22, 1967 Councilman Roger Fife introduced the following ordinance to concur with the new state law. The title of the ordinance read as follows:

AN ORDINANCE REGULATING HOURS FOR SALE OF ALCOHOLIC AND MALT BEVERAGES UNDER RETAIL LIQUOR LICENSES ISSUED BY THE CITY OF EVANSTON: AND REPEALING ORDINANCE NO. 133 AND ORDINANCE NO. 186 AND ANY AND ALL ORDINANCES OR PARTS OF ORDINANCES IN CONFLICT HEREWITH: AND DECLARING AN EMERGENCY.

This ordinance allowed the retail liquor dealers to stay open until 2:00 a.m. and to open at 6:00 a.m. every day of the week except Sunday, but it allowed them to be open on Sundays from 1:00 p.m. to 8:00 p.m. The ordinance also allowed the city council, during their January meeting of each year, to designate the dates of the four days that the ordinance would allow all liquor licensees the right to operate without restrictions as to closing hours: days like Cowboy Days, the Uinta County Fair, New Year's Eve and other types of celebrations that may come about.

After the ordinance was introduced the city council made a motion, with a second, to pass the ordinance on an emergency basis, meaning that if a motion is passed on the first reading it becomes law immediately. The vote on passing the ordinance on an emergency was passed by a split vote of the council.

When Mayor Burns called for a motion to pass the ordinance on first reading as an emergency, motion was made and seconded with a tied vote of 3-3, enabling the mayor to break the tie if he so desired. He did by voting in favor, causing the ordinance to pass on an emergency basis. Those voting in favor were Mayor Robert Burns, Councilmen James Smith, Roger Fife and me; those voting nay were Councilmen Arnold Christensen, William George and Melvin Baldwin.

During the time that Mayor Burns was in office, he refused to vote on any issues unless the vote was a tie and then he would vote to break the tie if he desired to, or he would leave the vote at a tie vote, causing the motion to fail.

The ordinance drew a lot of attention, mostly after it had passed. The editor and business manager Melvin Baldwin (also a city council member) of the Uinta County Herald made a big issue about the ordinance on the editorial page of the local newspaper. The editor spoke very much in opposition to the ordinance and he was very upset with the council for passing the ordinance on an emergency basis, though it was allowed through state law, when there was no rational reason for it except the local Liquor Dealers Association had requested it. When passing an ordinance on an emergency basis it only is presented to the public on one reading (hearing), while most ordinances go through three readings, giving the public more of a chance to be aware of the ordinance and have more time to study and think about the ordinance.

I believe, although at least two of the council members were strictly against the ordinance that maybe one of them would have voted in favor if it had not been done on an emergency status. I should have known better, but by being relatively new on the council I hadn't quite understood what passing an ordinance on emergency was all about, and there didn't seem to be any mention of it during the discussion among the council members. However, after thinking about it, I started wondering why the ordinance was such an emergency. There didn't seem to be any reason for it other than the liquor dealers wanted it passed that way.

I found out later that the real purpose of passing an ordinance on an emergency basis was when it concerned a health or safety problem, or any ordinance that may be necessary to bring into law immediately for the betterment of the community. Therefore, if I had given the ordinance more thought, I might not have voted for it unless it had time to go through the entire process of three readings. This would have given the public more time to read and understand the ordinance better and bring their pros and cons to the council. I probably would have voted in favor of it anyway, but it may have made the public feel better.

This was a learning experience for me. After that I was very careful when voting on any ordinance that came up on an emergency basis and allowing the city council to pass an ordinance on the first reading.

Evanston had a new nine-hole golf course that had been built by some of Evanston's golf enthusiasts. They acquired some land and immediately started clearing the brush, picking up rocks and laying out the course giving them a golf course with unimproved fairways and sand greens. The locals were proud of what they had done, but needed more funds to upgrade the course.

In 1966 they approached the previous administration for some help in funding to improve the course. At that time Mayor Raybourn and the city council told them that because it was a private course, the city by law could not assist them. The previous mayor and city council had told them that if they could lease the course back to the city so that it could become a public course, excluding the clubhouse that the group had obtained, there might be a possibility of the city applying for funds through the Wyoming Recreation Commission. The golf delegation then, after some lengthy discussion, agreed to lease the course back to the city and become a public golf course. The council passed a motion to enter into a lease to make the course available to the public without having to join the golf club. They had named the course the "Purple Sage Golf Course" and "The Purple Sage Golf Club", but the city would have no control over the club.

The same situation applied to the Eagle Rock Ski Hill when a group led by Kilburn Porter approached the previous administration to assist their group for finances to improve the ski hill. The Eagle Rock Ski Area was similar to the golf course situation. It had also been started and built by local ski enthusiasts. Unlike the golf course, it was already open to the public, but they needed funding to install a chair lift and other equipment to make it better and safer. Kilburn Porter actually spearheaded the project, but he had a lot of help from people like Rex Jones, Lamont Staley, Arden "Norm" Norman and many others, but like the golf course there was a lot that had to be done before the city could be involved.

The mayor and council told the ski hill organizers the same thing they told the golf club. Unless it was open to the public as a city-operated recreation area, by law the council could not give them any assistance. So, like the golf course, the council passed a motion to take over the ski hill group's leases. However, there were still resolutions and ordinances that had to be introduced and passed before the city could officially enter into any leases with the golf club or the ski hill.

At this time the mayor had assigned the six councilmen to oversee different departments. Because I had shown a lot of interest in recreation, Mayor Burns appointed me to oversee the city's recreation, parks and cemetery. This is where my interests were, and the golf course and the ski hill were two of the first projects that I would be involved with. It would be up to me to see that any grant application submitted for funding for any of our recreation or park projects was prepared and submitted to the Wyoming Recreation Commission.

The Wyoming Recreation Commission funds for grants were controlled and distributed through the Federal Land and Conservation Fund program. These funds were designated for recreation, including parks and playgrounds.

After applications were submitted we received funding from the Wyoming Recreation Commission in the amount of $6,867.00 for the ski hill in late December 1967, but it wasn't until February of 1968 that we received the funding for the golf course, in the amount of $9,921.379.

Making the course open to the public was a good idea. It gave everyone that wanted to the opportunity to play golf, plus it gave any person the opportunity to join the club if so desired. However, the number of citizens that cleaned up and cleared the area of all the rocks and brush and worked so hard building the course and ski area deserved a lot of credit.

I don't know whether or not it would have made any difference having a citizen from Evanston as a member on the Wyoming Recreation Commission, but it sure couldn't hurt. Governor Stan Hathaway was elected Governor of the State that election year. When he made his appointments to the various boards and commissions he appointed Albert Pilch from Evanston as a member of the Recreation Commission. I know Albert made a good pitch to the Commission for those golf course funds, and he helped Evanston a lot with other grants that we applied for.

At the time I went on the city council, the City of Evanston only had about three or four police officers, some only part time. There was only one police car that all officers used while on duty. Other than patrolling the town and walking through the bars once in a while, the police also door-checked every business in the city limits every night from the east end to the west end and north and south to make sure every door was safely locked. They quite often would find a door unlocked and then they would phone the proprietors and let them know that they had an unlocked door. This was one of the many public services they gave to the community during those days. This service is no longer available.

In 1966, Evanston School District #1 decided that they needed to build a new high school because the old high school would soon be condemned. The new school would be located off of Summit Street across from 4th Street where the baseball fields were. This was another project that came under my jurisdiction as councilman overseeing recreation and cemetery. It wasn't until 1967 that the school district accepted the plans and selected a contractor for the project. The city now had to find a new location for the baseball fields immediately, because the school would be starting construction soon.

The previous city administration had acted on a property trade with the school district in 1966, but had only passed a motion to trade property owned by the city. This city property was located at the end of 9th Street where the present Davis Middle School now stands. The school district owned the property where the new baseball field and tennis courts are presently located. The trade was made, everything worked out fine, and the city crews moved the baseball diamond to the new location right away so construction could start as soon as possible.

We had the baseball park ready to go by spring and the first director of the program that we hired was Harold "Hap" Fackrell. Hap had taught school at the Evanston Junior High School for a couple years after he got discharged from the service when the war ended. After leaving Evanston for a few years and then returning, he applied for the position and was hired.

After meeting Hap, it only took a short time to become good friends. He was one of those guys that once you shook hands you were no longer strangers. I had heard nothing but good about him so the council agreed to give him the job. He was only here for a couple years and then he moved to the Torrington area. But while he was in Evanston we got to be good friends.

That summer we also opened the swimming pool for the season, as we did every year.

After advertising for the pool supervisor we ended up hiring Patsy Madia for the season. She was a very competent swimmer and well qualified for the job. She supervised the swimming pool every summer for the next few years, and kept the pool and surrounding area very clean. She was also great with the kids and taught a lot of them how to swim.

The Anderson Park had previously been a housing complex called the V.F.W. Housing; some just called it the Vet's Village. The land was donated to the city by the owner, Waldemar Anderson. It was to be used for temporary housing for the veterans of World War II when they came home. In the mid-60s there was no longer a need for the housing, because most veterans used their G.I. bill to build homes of their own or others didn't care to live in that complex; it was getting pretty run down and the city was having trouble keeping it up. Finally the complex was condemned and demolished.

After the removal of the structures, for years the property was an empty lot and an unsightly weed patch. It was so bad that the neighbors began complaining, so the council applied for another small grant to get the area landscaped for a park. The application was also through the Wyoming Recreation Commission and was approved at the same time as the ski hill grant. The park was named in honor of the previous owner of the property, Mr. Anderson. We also got new tennis courts on the corner of Summit Street and 6th Street at that time, which was also accomplished through a recreation grant.

That same year, under my department, we were able to come up with some city money to build a nice brick and rod iron fence and entrance gate to the cemetery. The fence previously had been an old unsightly wire fence that just kept livestock out. The entrance to the cemetery was off County Road, which at that time was State Highway 89. The highway had a lot of traffic, so we wanted the cemetery to look nice as people drove by.

Mayor Burns was very concerned that Evanston had never had a zoning ordinance. This was one of his campaign promises, to enact an ordinance on planning and zoning, and I believe it was introduced by the council late in 1967, but wasn't passed until January 18, 1968. This was a first for the City of Evanston. It was the first time the city had ever been zoned. Some people didn't like it, but most understood that it was necessary. There were people that lived in the city limits who still had horses and other livestock, but they would still be legal because of what was called the "grandfather clause." With City Attorney Vehar's assistance, the zoning ordinance was prepared, introduced, and unanimously passed by the council on all three readings and enacted into law.

Mayor Burns also gave me the job as councilman to oversee Planning and Zoning and find someone to act as Evanston's first zoning and building inspector. This would only be a part time job. After advertising for someone, we hired Rod Blakeman. He had building experience, read the ordinance over, and assured us that he could do the job.

It was a tradition that the mayor and council honor all city employees by inviting them and their spouses to a year-end dinner. Some referred to it more as a Christmas dinner and party. Each employee also received a turkey or a ham for their family from the city. This was the mayor and council's way of thanking all of the city employees for doing such a good job throughout the year.

Well, this year was no different, except when the dinner was held in the large dining room of Freeman's Hotel, Mayor Burns decided that there would be a Happy Hour before dinner at the city's expense. This meant free drinks for all, but it got a little out of hand because some of the employees drank too many free drinks and were drunk before dinner even started. This upset quite a few council members and spouses. So from then on, this year-end event no longer had a free Happy Hour before dinner. We still had the bar, but everyone had to pay for their own drinks, which cut down the drinking considerably.

My first year as a member of the city council was a pretty busy year, but we now were going into the new year of 1968. From the looks of everything, we were looking to have a much busier year because there would be a lot of new construction, such as the sewer plant, new fire hall, the golf course, Anderson Park and the new high school.

CHAPTER 3

1968....The third and final reading on the zoning ordinance was passed unanimously by the council on January 18, 1968. A few weeks later, Mayor Burns asked the council for permission to form an official Planning and Zoning Board, as well as any suggestions on who might like to serve on the board. After some discussion of how many members there should be on the board, it was decided that the board should consist of nine members.

Each member would serve a three-year term. Three members would be either appointed or reappointed every three years. The mayor made these first appointments: For the one-year term, James "Jim" Marshall, Duane Shupe and Wayne Asay; for the two-year term, John Proffit, Eugene Jones and Harvey Johnston; and for the three-year term, Richard Bouck, Gene Nelson and Robert "Bob" Dickerson. After the one- and two-year terms were up they would be three-year appointments from then on.

Overseeing Planning and Zoning (P & Z) wasn't a great assignment to have, and I don't know why the mayor gave it to me. I never asked why, I accepted the position, but I did know that you don't make many friends when you are involved with telling people how and where they could build and locate.

One of the worst experiences I had was when a couple of motel owners, Dub Mills of the Dunmar Best Western Motel, and John Grove of the Hillcrest Motel were having a dispute. Mills didn't want Grove to build an extension on the east end of his motel because he was afraid it would stick out too far towards the road and would hide his establishment from highway traffic from the west.

When the board was notified of the situation they instructed Rod Blakeman, our inspector, to go and check out the situation and measure the distance where the property owner was going to start his building and how close to the highway it would be. I believe at that time a commercial building had to be 20 feet in from the boundary of the highway right-of-way. Blakeman declared, after measuring, that Grove was within the law and had every right to proceed. Mr. Mills was so upset that he went to the city attorney's office, Mr. Vince Vehar, and complained to him. Vehar explained that I was the councilman overseeing P & Z and that he should talk to me. So Mills sent his son, Paul, up to the truck stop where I was working and had him ask me to come down to Vehar's office where Mills was. When I got there, Mills very nicely asked me to do something to stop Grove from building the addition to his motel. I told him that the inspector measured the distance from the highway and verified that Grove was within the zoning law, and that I would not tell Grove that he could not build his addition.

We discussed it for a while and I listened to Mills's concern, but he didn't argue with me or give me any good reason where Grove was out of order. When the Mills group left, appearing to still be friendly. I explained my position to Vehar and he agreed with me. I don't know whether or not the mayor heard anything about this dispute or not, but I never heard another word about it.

I felt bad about the entire mess, but Dub Mills and his son Paul and I got to be good friends. They knew if the situation was reversed I would have done the same for them. They just treated me as if nothing had happened. I guess Mills felt that he at least had to try, and I couldn't blame him for that. I might have done the same if I had been in his shoes. This was quite an experience for me, one that I wasn't expecting and didn't particularly care for. It was my first experience of this type, but it sure wouldn't be the last.

The new freeway, Interstate 80, was scheduled to be completed and would go around Evanston with off ramps and exits to the town at the west end and the east end. This was causing big changes in our commercial areas; new motels, service stations, restaurants and bars were being built closer to the off ramps. This gave the city some additional financial problems because we had to annex and extend the city limits, requiring extensions of water and sewer lines. A zoning ordinance was definitely needed at this time

When they surveyed for the Interstate around the community, through the condemnation act, the Wyoming Highway Department had to relocate a few residences that were on the hill at the far south-east end of Main Street off 1st Street. This is where the Hughes family lived. Mr. Glen Hughes and some of his family came to a council meeting quite concerned, which was very understandable, about what was to happen to them and their homes. The mayor and council were also concerned and were very much aware of their situation, so they requested that a representative from the Wyoming Highway Department be at that meeting.

After a considerable amount of discussion, the highway department explained why they had to relocate them and assured the Hughes that they would either be bought out at a fair price, or they could be relocated to another house if that was what they wanted. Glen Hughes was relocated to a house near the same area at 100 Main Street. The house appeared to be just as nice or nicer and Hughes appeared to be well satisfied.

The freeway was completed and opened up in 1968, and it changed the community tremendously. There was far less traffic coming into town and going through the town on old U.S. Highway 30 S, so downtown Evanston became much quieter. This was such a big change that some of the business owners were forced to make adjustments to meet the change, while others shut completely down. Evanston at this time had a population of about 3,800 and was relatively stable, but the future would bring more problems.

The business owners on the west end of the city were quite concerned about the location of the west-bound traffic's off ramp from the freeway.

Some wanted it closer toward town near Lombard Street while others wanted it at the city limits, which is where it is at present, and some wanted it even further west.

Back then the city limits were between the Standard Service Station, now known as Anderson's Standard, and where the truck stop was located. The truck stop was owned by Husky Oil Company (formerly Frontier) at the time the freeway went around the city and was located originally on the south side of U.S. Highway 30 S, now known as Harrison Drive. The south side of U.S. Highway 30 S marked the southern limit of Evanston, and on the north side the city ended just before the street presently known as 19th Street. Just a few years before the freeway, I-80 went around Evanston, our company distributer, Otto Kennedy, purchased five acres across the highway from where our Husky truck stop was. A few years after I-80 was completed around the city, Husky Oil Company purchased the land from Kennedy and built a new truck stop. Several years later Husky Oil sold out to "Flying J," where it is located today.

A few years before the freeway was opened, Frank Woolley, an Evanston business man, purchased a large piece of property on the west end of Evanston, including both sides of U.S. Highway 30 S. This property extended from the truck stop on the south side of old U.S. Highway 30 S across the interstate, including some property south of the freeway and the north side of U.S. Highway 30 S. The area extended from the property that Otto Kennedy had purchased (where Flying "J" is located today), west to the end of the section line near Hampton Inn, and up to the golf course property where Altitude Motors and West View Village are now located.

Mr. Woolley owned Wooley's Automotive Supply in Evanston, located on the corner of 11th Street and Main, later becoming Kallas Automotive Supply, and where Uinta Realty, Inc. is currently located. Woolley loved Evanston and had big plans for the property he had purchased, but he resided in Ogden, Utah. He told me that he would move to Evanston in a minute, but his wife, Mickey, wouldn't leave Ogden.

After Mr. Woolley purchased the property, he petitioned the Evanston City Council for annexation of the entire property he had purchased, plus Mr. Kennedy's property. He explained to the council what his plans were: He would first build a Ramada Inn motel, a restaurant called the F Bar M, and two service stations, one on each side of U.S. Highway 30 S. These would be built immediately.

He then planned to construct an Old West style fort with high walls and make it into an amusement place that would attract tourists, and where families with kids could come and enjoy themselves. He also talked about other attractions that he had planned, which would give more reasons for freeway traffic to stop in Evanston and spend some time here. His plans sounded great and after more discussion concerning water, sewer and other services, he told us that he would take care of most of that in his construction and guaranteed that they would be built according to city specifications. Woolley finished the construction of the Ramada Inn in early 1969 and started his other projects. Mr. Blaine Sanders was Woolley's general foreman of all this construction, including the Ramada. They also completed the F Bar M café and the two service stations. One was branded Chevron and the other was branded Sinclair. Both are still in business, but the Sinclair has since changed to Shell Oil.

Frank Woolley was a good and well informed business person and kept up with a lot of programs that would help the economy. He called for a meeting with some of the business owners. He had learned about a new program that the U.S. Small Business Administration (S.B.A.) had introduced, called the 502 Loan Program. The S.B.A. 502 plan was a participatory program that was considered a 10/40/50 plan for the entity (borrower) participating with 10% of the funds and the development company, with an S.B.A. guarantee of 40% of the funding, plus the lender (bank) would participate with the addition 50%. The bank or lender would hold first mortgage. It was a good program for a borrower, and with the S.B.A. guarantee, it appeared to be favorable with the lenders.

Woolley explained that the program had to be administered through a non-profit development company board of directors made up of five to nine members, who had to be local people. Loans would be made to new or existing businesses that qualified. Our first step would be to organize the board by voting on how many members and who was to serve.

The G.E.D.C. was a nonprofit organization formed by the local citizens with the intention of bringing new industry and businesses to

Evanston and the area to help better the economy. To be a member of it you had to buy stock so that the company would have some operating funds. No one could buy more than $200.00 worth of stock and no one could have a controlling interest in the company.

During this meeting I was one of the members nominated and voted on, along with 8 others. I also nominated by Woolley to become the first president of the board. The vote was unanimous. The board incorporated under the business name The Greater Evanston Development Company, Inc. (G.E.D.C.). I ended up serving on the board as president for the next 21 years.

1968 turned out to be a very busy year for the city, with all the construction and annexation of properties. This was my second year as a member of the city council and I was still councilman overseeing recreation, parks, and cemetery, and in addition I now had the thankless job of Planning and Zoning.

Being president of the G.E.D.C. shouldn't have taken up too much of my time—except for getting organized. I didn't know what to expect or how much of my time the company would take. There wasn't anyone beating at the bush to use the program at this time except Frank Woolley, who was in the process of developing his property.

At this time James "Jim" Smith was retiring from his business and had decided to resign from the council. Jim had been a councilman for quite some time and had served the city very well. He owned the Smith Transportation Company, which contracted with the school district each year to bus the school kids to and from school, athletic events and other activity trips out of town; but he had now sold the business to Miles Alexander of the Alexander Motel.

The mayor and council had accepted Smith's resignation with some reservations and regrets, but immediately had the city clerk put out the necessary advertising to fill Smith's vacant Ward 2 council seat. The appointment would only be until the next general election. Two people applied; Russell "Bub" Albrecht and Royce Bills. The vote would be at the next regular council meeting

During the meeting, by a split vote, Albrecht was voted on to serve on the council in place of Smith until the next general election, which would be in November of that year, 1968. 1968 was a presidential election year and Evanston had three councilmen up for re-election; the three would be Mel Baldwin, Arnold Christensen and Bill George, plus Albrecht would also have to run.

Also in 1968, the State of Wyoming legalized parimutuel betting for horseracing, but each county in the state had to vote on whether they wanted it legal in their county. Some folks in Uinta County petitioned the county commissioners to hold an election concerning parimutuel betting. The commission agreed to hold elections in April of 1968.

The Evanston Chamber of Commerce, among other organizations, endorsed the right to have parimutuel betting, thinking it would help the town's commercial industry. It wasn't too long after the law came into effect that they started horseracing at the fairgrounds in Evanston with parimutuel betting, but it would be quite a few years before a regular horseracing establishment was constructed anywhere in the county.

The election had been held in the county, and the parimutuel bill had passed, but only by 14 votes. This was a big surprise for most, because with all the support in favor of the bill, we thought that it would pass by a landslide.

Among other programs and projects that we had going this year, it was also Evanston's Centennial, as well as the Union Pacific Railroad's Centennial. The City of Evanston had planned their schedule of centennial events from July 1 through July 6.

In May of that year the U.P. Reclamation Plant superintendent presented the City of Evanston with a beautiful Centennial Plaque. Other local committees and organizations also had programs going on during the year in honor of the Centennial; for instance, the Evanston Jaycees had their beard-growing contest. I don't remember who won, but there were a lot of men in Evanston walking around with beards. It was a fun time.

The railroad had their big celebration of "Railroad Days" scheduled for July 20th. A lot of U.P. dignitaries were on hand to congratulate Evanston, and took time out to talk to some of the U.P. employees. Part of their celebration continued into 1969!

Every year in the spring and summer, the City of Evanston would start running short on water. We were very concerned about the golf course so we decided to drill a well on the course just for its use. But it didn't work out that way—we ended up putting the course well into the main line in case the public needed more water.

Evanston received most of their water out of Bear River. We had an intake off the Bear about 12 miles south of Evanston, but when the irrigators, who also used water out of the Bear, started irrigating through the growing season, the river got pretty low. When this happened the city became short on water and we had to use some of the city wells. Evanston, including the golf course well, had several operating wells around town. Some were much better than others. Our best wells were located at the Anderson Park, and where the Jubilee Shopping Center parking lot is at present, which at that time was railroad property. We also had a good well located near the rodeo and fair grounds. We had wells at the cemetery and a couple others that weren't too good, but were usable when needed. Almost every year, because of the shortage, we had no other choice than to ration water. The procedure during those times was to put the public on a plan where they could only water their yards every other day. Normally we used odd and even house numbers, where the homes with odd numbered house addresses could water on odd numbered days and even numbers on the opposite days. This meant people could water no more than every other day, but some years when we were especially short on water, we allowed the public to water only between the evening hours from 6:00 p.m. to 9:00 p.m. It just depended on how short we were on water.

There was no doubt that we had a water problem and if the town ever had an increase in population we would be in big trouble. Therefore, the mayor and council were also working on enlarging the water plant that was on the hill just to the south of town that we call the "E" Hill. The "E" represents Evanston High School.

At this time, there was a big demand from the public to add fluoridation to our water supply. Several proponents of this plan came to one of our meetings and gave us their reasoning behind the idea.

After hearing all the pros and cons for the next several weeks, the council made a motion at their August 5th meeting requesting the Wyoming State Health Department to do a survey of the city's water supply to determine the needed equipment and the cost to install a fluoridation system. The motion was seconded and passed unanimously, but it would be years before anything would be done about it; there were also people who were very much against it. It was going to be very controversial, and I was not looking forward to it.

The new Evanston High School was under construction by the Skyline of Wyoming Construction Company, the low bidder, but wouldn't be completed and ready for students to move into until late in January 1969. When it was ready, the school district had a big open house, and then the high school kids started moving into their new school, which had a nice gym and a regulation swimming pool.

My oldest son, Randy, and my niece, Shelley Hutchings, were both seniors at that time and would be among the first group of kids to graduate from the new school that spring. I believe it was the largest class yet to have graduated from Evanston High School with 102 graduates.

The golf course, after receiving the grants from the Wyoming Recreation Commission, now had new greens and fairways and was looking good. Fifty-six spruce trees had been planted in 1967; they were looking great and they added a lot to the course.

The new fire hall located on the corner of Center and 8th Street was completed. An open house was held on November 16, 1968 with Mayor Burns and Chief Jones giving short speeches. The old fire station had been in the old town hall and didn't have enough room for more than one piece of equipment. The old fire station was turned into a museum at the request of a group of interested folks.

Other projects that were getting some improvements that year through grants from the Recreation Commission were the tennis courts, Anderson Park, Eagle Rock Ski area, and the North Park located on the corner of Avenue A and Second Avenue in North Evanston. Also, the Purple Sage Golf Club received a Federal Housing Administration (F.H.A.) loan in the amount of $35,000.00 and broke ground for a new clubhouse.

Other issues that came up during the year were the downtown parking problem, which caused the council to authorize some additional parking meters, and the terms and conditions of the franchise agreements to utility companies that authorized the use of city streets and alleys for their lines. Some of these agreements were about to expire and become due for renewal soon. Also, the problem of new water line extensions had to be considered, and, of course, the dog problem came up again as usual. The dog problem was always one of Evanston biggest problems and hardest to control, but with the nearby sheep and livestock ranches, something had to be done about them. At that time we couldn't afford an animal control officer or a building to keep them in, so our police department had to handle all calls and do the best they could with what we had.

The general election was held in November and all three regular councilmen got re-elected, but councilman Albrecht, who was appointed to fill a vacancy, lost his re-election bid to Royce Bills. We would be going into the next year with one new member on the council, Mr. Bills.

We had our year-end Christmas dinner for the employees again that year. It turned out to be a good evening and a swell dinner. No one got out of order and I believe everyone had a good time.

CHAPTER 4

1969-1970....I was now in my third year, 1969, as a member of the city council. I had felt good about the past two years, and through the efforts of many, the city had made a lot of progress and accomplished many goals. In addition to everything else, the city had now taken over the golf course and ski hill, which I felt would be a good addition to our overall recreation program, but it would have a big effect on the city's budget. We would also still have other problems to be concerned about, such as our water problem. We would more than likely have to ration water usage again this coming summer and we would have the big issue of fluoridation come up again sometime in the next few years.

At the first meeting of the year, Mayor Burns had City Clerk Percy Hudson swear in the newly re-elected council members, Baldwin, Christensen and George, plus our new member, Royce Bills. The mayor then continued to make his usual appointments, adding the position of City Engineer. He re-appointed John Proffit, of Proffit Engineering, as engineer. With the construction of the sewer plant starting up and with several other projects that would be going on, Proffit was going to have plenty to do.

Mayor Burns once again assigned me to Recreation as well as Planning and Zoning, but he gave the cemetery to Royce Bills, which didn't hurt my feelings one bit. The main reason Burns gave Bills the cemetery was because Bills was very interested in the city initiating a perpetual care program, and the appointment fit right in with what he was trying to do.

The perpetual care program was a good idea and the mayor and council agreed to act on it immediately to make it into law. The program would require that each person who had purchased a lot or plot of lots in the past, or would be purchasing in the future, pay a one-time fee to the city for perpetual care for each lot. Through his efforts, the program was unanimously adopted and made into law by the council. The fee would be a one-time cost of $25.00 for the city to care for the lots forever. I'm not sure what the fee is today, but over the years, it has turned out to be a great program. Evanston has always had a nice and well-kept cemetery because of it. Rod Blakeman would remain our inspector for planning and zoning for another year, and the new budget didn't change much from previous years, except we needed to make some adjustments to include the golf course and ski hill. Evanston had purchased a snow packer that winter, which wasn't a budget item for that particular year, so we took it out of the budget elsewhere.

In the past we had talked quite a bit about trying to get a chair lift for the Eagle Rock Ski Hill. That winter of 1969 and 1970 Kilburn Porter found out that a ski area located in Provo Canyon in Utah, called Timp Haven, had just put in a new chair lift and that they might sell their old one pretty cheap.

When Porter informed Mayor Burns about the lift they both thought it was worth looking into, so they invited Rex Jones and me to take a trip with them to Timp Haven, now known as the Sundance Ski area, owned by the actor Robert Redford. After lunch, we finally got to meet with the owner. He told us that he wanted $5,000.00 for the lift, but we told him the city could not afford that much. So Mayor Burns offered him $3,000.00, plus we would furnish the transportation to pick up the lift and haul it to Evanston. The owner finally agreed, and we told him that if the city council agreed to the purchase, our city crew would come to load it up and take it to Evanston. The owner then suggested to us that we should get hold of the person that installed their new lift and talk to him about the possibility of installing our lift. Since the same guy took down the lift, he knew what was there. So the owner gave the mayor the name and telephone number of the installation person so we could see what he would charge to install our "new" used chair lift.

After closing the deal, we had an enjoyable day of skiing, I hadn't learned to ski yet, and I wasn't planning on doing any skiing that particular day, but my friends had other plans for me. The other three decided they wanted to go up on the chair lift and ski down the highest ski run. Well, as I had never had any experience skiing, I was just planning on waiting for them, but Porter rented me some ski boots, poles and skis and talked me into giving it a try. He said it was time for me to learn how to ski if I was to be involved with the ski hill. So they got me on Timp Haven's new chair lift and took me up to the highest damn hill, and then they helped me put on my skis and told me how to ski and what to do going down the hill. They said they would all stay behind me and keep an eye out if I needed help. Well, that was a stupid thing to say because they knew I would need help and they never stayed behind me, but they did keep coming up on the lift and skiing down past me to make sure I was all right. After about a dozen falls and about an hour later, I did finally make it to the bottom. It was a fun day, but I didn't really enjoy my first time skiing.

When we got back to Evanston, Mayor Burns immediately called the contractor, who had installed the new lift at Timp Haven, and told him that we were in the process of trying to buy Timp Haven's old lift and explained to him our situation. After asking him if he would be interested in constructing it, he said that his company would be glad to install the lift. He said that he would get back to us with a cost. The contractor was Ray Crandall from the Inter-mountain Ski Lift Company. I don't recall what he quoted, but during the next meeting, the mayor got council approval to purchase the lift and also to enter into a contract with Randall's company to construct the lift. We didn't put it out for bid because there was no one else around that had the experience of installing chair lifts. The council voted unanimously in favor, and in addition we were able to get a grant from the Recreation Commission to help pay for it. Construction began that summer and the lift was completed the next January.

In February 1969 we opened the bids for a new sewer plant. The lowest bid was just under $129,000. After all the advertisements that the law required concerning the sale of the bonds and grants we received from the state, the project got under way. The plant was completed in November of 1969, finally getting the Utah and Wyoming agencies off our back now that we were no longer dumping raw sewage into the Bear River.

That year the state legislature passed a law that 18- through 20-year-olds could legally drink beer as long it was not more than 3.3% alcohol. This caused a lot of problems throughout the state because of the difficulty of bar operators trying to control what youngsters under 21 years of age would be drinking, and it caused problems for the police as well. (A few years later, the state changed the law back to what it was previously.) The state legislature also passed an increase in the minimum wage that year—to $1.30 per hour.

We also received another grant that year from the recreation commission to finish up the improvements to Anderson Park, and we were able to finish the improvements on North Park in North Evanston.

The State of Wyoming announced that they would be building a new armory in Evanston. The old armory was built back in 1950 and was in need of repair and improvement. The City of Evanston owned some property at the southeast end of Sage and Summit Streets, which the state department decided would be the site for the new armory. Early in the year the state purchased the property from the city and in September of 1969 they had a groundbreaking ceremony.

The old armory was located on 6th Street, near where the baseball fields and the skateboard rink are presently located. It was built only as temporary metal building and was never meant to be permanent. It was built for Company "A", a medium tank unit, of the 141st Tank Battalion of the Wyoming National Guard. It wasn't built with high warehouse doors where you could drive a tank or any other army vehicle inside. It had a small office, a classroom and a hall for drills. It was built only as a temporary structure, and after about 20 years it started having a lot of problems and was in such disrepair that the Wyoming National Guard tore it down and gave the property to the city.

I had joined that unit of the Wyoming National Guard in November of 1949 when I was 17 years old. We were meeting at the old American Legion Hall located at 1025 Sage Street at the time, which has since been made into a residence. The old armory wasn't built until 1950, not too long before the 141st Tank Battalion was activated for the Korean War in September of 1950.

The new armory was being built for the use of an artillery outfit and was much larger so they could get large military vehicles inside. It was also built as a permanent structure and is still in use.

A big problem we had in the spring of 1969 was that the river got so high it flooded a lot of homes in the North Evanston area. It was so bad that the State of Wyoming Department of Environmental Quality and the U.S. Army Corps of Engineers were called in. After they looked the problem over, they met with the city council to determine what to do to prevent this from happening again in the future. They said there would be a study done by the state and this would be completed sometime in the next year.

The study didn't get completed until the following year, but it indicated that dikes on both sides of the river should be installed from the County Road river bridge to the end of 2nd Avenue. This would be done at the expense of the federal government. Their big problem would be getting access to the river bank. For this, they needed the city's assistance talking to the various property owners to allow the corps access through their properties to build the dikes along the river. After a period of time, with some static from some of the property owners, the corps finished the project the summer of 1970.

I was still in charge of the Little League Football Program—not necessarily by choice, it just turned out that way. I kept it going and stayed with it because I felt that it was a worthwhile program for young boys, and didn't want to see it stopped. I was grateful to Russell "Bub" Albrecht for his efforts in getting the Evanston Quarterback Club to adopt and sponsor the program. At least now I wouldn't have to be worrying about raising finances any more to keep the program going. However, they wanted me to still be in charge. I told them that I would accept the assignment again that year, but I didn't want to commit for years to come.

In late October, the Union Pacific Railroad requested from the federal transportation department the right to stop some of their passenger trains from running through Wyoming. This created concern among the locals that this was just the beginning of a lot of changes that would be happening in the U.P. system and which would have an enormous effect on Evanston's economy, and because of the changes, it did have.

That fall the issue of running snow machines on the golf course during winter months came up in the council. Mayor Burns was in favor of allowing the machines on the course. There were snow machine activists and members of the golf club at the meeting. Mr. Evan Reese was leading the snow machine group and the mayor was speaking in their favor. He looked at the golf course as a recreation area and believed that it should be used for multiple purposes. But the council was very much concerned about the greens on the course. It wasn't very long since the greens were put in, and we didn't want them damaged by someone driving a snow machine over them. The snow machine group assured us that they would mark the greens and keep their machines in the rough and the fairways. However, the council was also concerned about who was going to police the situation. There was no way that anyone could control the traffic of the machines, especially after dark. Besides, they were also concerned about the fairways now that they had new grass.

Therefore, the council voted unanimously against allowing any type of machines or vehicles on the course other than those related to golf. They felt that it was a golf course and that's only what it should be used for. The mayor accepted the council's decision and nothing more was said.

Also, late that fall, Mayor Burns brought up issues concerning the airport: the problems that we had in keeping a qualified manager, and the possibility of finding a new location for it. They needed a new site because when taking off to the north or landing from the north, the hills were too close to the airport for safety. In the past some pilots had had problems gaining enough altitude to clear the hills on take-off, sometimes causing accidents.

Mayor Burns suggested to the council that we form an airport board as soon as possible because he believed that it would help

Evanston in receiving assistance from the Wyoming Aeronautics Commission. He said any funding we applied for would be mostly federal money, but would have to come through the state commission to be administered. Therefore, after more discussion, the motion to form such a board was made and seconded with all voting in favor. The mayor suggested the following members: Dr. S. L. Ekins, Roy Turner, Donald Barnard, Blaine Sanders and Lee Guild. With the council's approval the board was formed.

That winter of 1969 and 1970 was a very cold winter and in January a lot of pipes froze in houses. Earlier, the city had put up notices that the municipality would not be responsible for any freeze-ups or broken pipes. They advised that on below-freezing nights, people should open their taps and allow a small stream of water to flow to keep the pipes from freezing, especially if their water taps were located on an outside wall. Some people didn't listen and consequently had quite a few freeze-ups and broken pipes.

That winter the city council also passed an ordinance restricting over-the-snow vehicles in the town limits. People were running their snow machines over private and public property, causing a lot of damage in different areas. Therefore, the council felt that they had no other choice than to adopt some restrictions.

Some of the Planning and Zoning Board members' terms expired and they came up for renewal. Those re-appointed were Gene Nelson and John Proffit. New appointments made after some previous members had resigned were Councilman William George, Lamar Day of Utah Power and Light and Sherman Ryan of Mountain States Telephone. I was still councilman overseeing P & Z.

The new sewer plant was finished and that spring the public was invited to inspect and get a first-hand look at the finished project. There weren't many people present, but those that were there were quite impressed by it. But it wouldn't be long before Evanston, as it grew, would need a much bigger plant, especially if it grew very fast—and it did.

However, in May of 1970 the census bureau announced a drop in population for Evanston. According to them we now had a population of approximately 4,000. That was about a 10 to 15 percent decline.

Other projects that went on that summer were diking the river banks under the supervision of the U.S. Army Corps of Engineers. A new maintenance building at the cemetery was built by Barnes Construction. Uinta County and the City of Evanston worked on a plan for civil defense with Director Bernard Gram (Gram had been appointed Director of Civil Defense at the time the program began shortly after World War II). We also hired new police officers and purchased a couple of new police cars during that year, and the fire department purchased a rural type fire truck to be used outside the city for brush fires and so on.

That April, the city council had a special meeting to discuss a petition presented by a number of property owners for the city to consider an improvement district where their streets could be improved with pavement and curb and gutters. At this time Evanston had many unimproved streets and the city was trying to get certain areas of streets improved through Improvement District Programs. All owners in the district would have the opportunity to vote for or against the petition. To pass the petition would require that a majority of the property owners vote in favor before the city could pass the resolution to apply for the bonding. Once the bonds were sold and the improvement district was complete, each property owner in that district would pay an assessment every year to pay off the bonds for however long it took. The vote by the property owners was overwhelmingly in favor. So we had a big street project ahead of us that summer if we got the bonds sold.

Hap Fackrell, who had been in charge of our summer baseball program for the past couple of years, was not going to be doing it this year. He was leaving Evanston for another teaching job elsewhere in the state. He did a great job for us and the kids loved him, but now we had to find someone else. Fortunately, that didn't take long. Phil Peterson was hired for the job of coach and director of the program. He held the job for the next few years and also did a good job with the kids. I don't recall how long he held the position, but I was sure glad to have him.

In our May meeting, before passing the new budget, the council raised the mayor's salary to $2,400.00 per year and the city councilman's to $900.00 per year. However, neither the mayor nor the members of the council that were up for re-election this year of 1970 would receive the increase unless they were re-elected. Also, the other three holdover council members would not receive the increase until the next election, which wouldn't be until 1972, assuming they ran successfully again. By law, elected city officials can vote themselves a raise in wages while in office, but cannot receive that raise until after their next election, providing they run again and win.

We also voted to give city workers who had been employed by the City of Evanston for at least 13 years an annual two-week paid vacation starting January 1, 1971. This would be the first time any of the city employees had received any type of benefit.

Once in a while, some may have received a raise based on their position, but that was all. It would be years before they would receive any other benefits such as health insurance, retirement plan and a decent schedule of vacation time and reasonable wages. I believe at that time they were probably the lowest-paid group in the area.

That summer, Evanston was scheduled to have a new water intake constructed on the upper Bear River. The old intake was wearing out and needed to be replaced. During the construction, the city could not receive any water from the river. Therefore, we had to start up every well in the city that was good enough for culinary purposes, including the golf course well. Throughout that summer, we had to ration water by putting folks on the odd and even day schedule for watering their yards, from 6:00 p.m. to 9:00 p.m.

The budget that was passed for the next fiscal year of 1970-1971 was just under $340,000 for the general fund and $97,000 for the water fund. Once again, we had to cut back on certain things to make the budget balance, but it was that way every year for quite some time. By law, a municipality, either town or city, had to have their budget balanced every year, or they would be subject to a penalty and fine, plus possible criminal action, very much unlike the federal government.

At that time, most of Evanston was on the UHF television system. This was another project that Kilburn Porter had instigated. He formed a nonprofit company called Upper Bear River TV, Inc. His group did this through donations rather than by charging fees, but after a couple years they were having a hard time getting people to give donations. They did get enough donations and other assistance to get the tower up and the system going, but soon had to turn to the city for financial help or start assessing those that were connected to the system. The only other system that we had, at that time, were the roof antennas attached to each house.

When Porter and his advocates approached the mayor and council for assistance we informed them that we could not assist the company at that time. We explained that our new budget for the next fiscal year had been advertised and passed by the council and there was not going to be enough funding for broadcasting unless we could sponsor a grant for it, but Porter explained that they had already tried for a grant and had gotten turned down. The group did finally get some more donations to keep the system going for a while longer. At that time it was the best television available.

Kilburn Porter was one of the boating enthusiasts that played a big role in getting the boat club started. After the Sulphur Creek Reservoir was completed, it sparked a lot of interest in fishing, boating, water skiing and surfboarding. Porter and other boat lovers started a boat club. The other members I recall were James "Buff" Bruce and Bob Mathson. I'm sure there were many more because boating got very popular at that time. Porter put me on my first surfboard and water skis.

Kilburn did an awful lot of good for recreation in the Evanston area. He was the big organizer for Eagle Rock Ski Area, he helped in the little league football, he was the big gun for the UHF television system and he was instrumental in making boating sports popular at Sulphur Creek Reservoir.

On October 15, 1970, the Wyoming National Guard completed the new armory and they dedicated it on that day. It was named in honor of former M/Sgt. Francis T. "Pappy" Taylor, top sergeant of the motor pool of Company "A" of the 141st Tank Battalion before and during the time the unit served in the Korean War. It was a great, well-deserved honor for him and his family. The dedication marked the time of Pappy Taylor's retirement. His son Ted Taylor served time in Korea while his father was active in the states.

1970 was an election year, and my term in office was coming to an end, as were those of Mayor Burns, Roger Fife and Royce Bills. May 20, 1970 was the opening date for filing for office and the deadline was sometime in July, but Fife and I both immediately filed for re-election. Mayor Burns and Bills waited until sometime in July to file, but both ended up filing for re-election. Others that had filed for mayor were Fire Chief Edward Jones, former Mayor Harold Raybourn and former councilman Russell "Bub" Albrecht. Bills and I were unopposed. Fife of Ward 3 had two people file against him, Ronald Davis and Clarence Bateman.

During the primary election the two top winners for mayor were Mayor Burns and Edward Jones. Bills and I were unopposed so we were almost automatically elected. Fife and Davis won the primary for Ward 3. Then came the general election, and Mayor Burns was re-elected along with Bills and me. Davis won the seat from Fife, so now we would have another new member of the council.

My first full term of four years had been a very busy time and one hell of a learning period. It seemed that we got a lot done, but there were still problems, some that could be very controversial, such as fluoridation. We also had concerns about the city dumps. The order to stop burning at the dumps came from the state, so that was something we would have to be looking at in the next few years, trying to locate a new landfill site. Also, there was always the dog problem. With the city budget it was tough to get all these problems taken care of, but we would just have to wait and see what the next four years would bring.

CHAPTER 5

1971....I was now going into my second term as a member of the Evanston City Council and I was looking forward to it. But looking back at the past four years, my thoughts were that we did get a hell of a lot accomplished. I also feel that the next term will be just as busy. With all the cutbacks that the railroad was anticipating, the Evanston water situation, and many other problems, including the subject of fluoridation coming up once again, I was sure we were looking at another very busy four years. One of our main concerns was the economy.

With Mayor Burns, Bills and me getting re-elected, the council hadn't changed much. Though Fife lost to Ron Davis in Ward 3, we still had the remaining council members, Baldwin, Christensen and George on board. With Ron Davis now on the council, we knew that there would be a lot of discussion concerning fluoridation in the water. He was one of the main opponents against fluoridation. Until then, the council had never taken any action on the subject. I don't think there had been much interest in it as far as the council had been concerned.

On Tuesday, January 5, 1971, we were all sworn in again, plus Ron Davis for the first time. Percy Hudson, City Clerk, once again did the swearing in. Following the swearing-in ceremony, Mayor Burns made his usual appointments and then his selection of what departments each member of the council would be responsible for. He kept me in Parks and Recreation, which I appreciated. He assigned Bill George to water and sewer in addition to the Planning and Zoning Board. Arnold Christensen was chosen to oversee the street department; Royce Bills the cemetery, and Mel Baldwin and Ron Davis were jointly instructed to oversee the sanitation department and the airport. They were also asked by the mayor to head up a study of the ecology of the city and the immediate area.

The new improved Eagle Rock Ski Area opened up on Sunday, January 10, 1971. The new chair lift was finished and operating, and the rope tows were serviced and ready for operation. User's fees were set for both the chair lift and rope tows as follows: Chair lift for adults was $3.00 for full day and $2.00 for half day, and for kids under the age of 12 the fee was $2.00 for full day and $1.50 for half day. The rope tows for adults were $2.25 for full day and $1.75 for half day, and kids under the age of 12 were $1.75 for full day and $1.25 for half day. Opening day turned out to be a big day for skiers. There was a big crowd and everyone was having a great time. I believe every kid from the area learned to ski at Eagle Rock.

We had another very serious dog problem that month. On Saturday, January 9, 1971 a large pack of marauding dogs killed about a dozen head of sheep in a pasture at a local ranch near the edge of Evanston. We'd always had dog problems, but this time the mayor and city council realized just how serious things were, so we talked about hiring an animal control officer and the possibility of finding a place for a dog pound. This wasn't easy to cure because of lack of funds in the budget, but we did work out a program. It was not really satisfactory, but it was better than ignoring the situation. As funds became available, the program got much better.

During the first part of February, Engineer John Proffit and Mr. Frank Woolley presented a proposed plat of a new subdivision. The subdivision would be called the Country Club Estates. Very impressed, we directed Mr. Woolley to present his plan to the Planning and Zoning Board for their recommendations. Mr. Woolley planned to do a lot of developing in the city, and I thought it was good that someone still had a lot of faith in our community.

Mr. Woolley was also owner of Woolley's Automotive Supply, located at 1049 Main Street. He decided that as he had so much going on, he would sell the company to his oldest employee, Fred Kallas. Fred had been employed by Woolley since 1949 and knew the business very well. The store became Kallas Automotive Supply. Woolley also was the owner of a large shopping center in Ogden that he was building a large addition onto. This center in Ogden kept him so busy that he didn't have enough time to spend in Evanston. He brought in Blaine Sanders from Ogden to take over his projects in Evanston. Sanders would not only be his construction supervisor for the construction of the Ramada Inn and the F Bar M Restaurant, he also would take over the management of both establishments.

Sanders and I became good friends, and we worked together improving the economy of Evanston. He was one of the board members of The Greater Evanston Development Company and took a serious interest in the community. I will never forget when he went out of his way to save the used bars of soap from his motel rooms and brought them to us at the truck stop to use in our truck driver showers. It saved us from having to buy any. Some drivers had their own soap, but it was there in case they didn't. Anyway, we appreciated Sanders' generosity.

The Eagle Rock Ski Hill had a competitive ski meet on February 7th, which was a big success. They had a great turnout of skiers competing, and a large crowd of spectators. It turned out to be a very successful event. Skiing got so popular at that time that Evanston High even incorporated it into their athletic program and had ski teams that competed with other schools.

The 1970s was a time period when the entire country was having a lot of problems with our young people using a lot of illegal drugs: marijuana, cocaine, and so on. This was a time during the period of the very unpopular Vietnam War. Washington seemed to be sending the wrong message to our young people, causing the country to have these problems, and the sale and use of drugs were a big concern. Evanston was no different, so Mayor Burns formed what he called a Drug Commission. He assigned my wife Sandy, Russell "Bub" and Charles Albrecht, Chief of Police Chuck Overy, Charles and Dorothy Bright, Robert Holmes and others that I don't quite recall. The purpose of the commission was to complete a study to find out the best ways to combat the problem and how to handle those kids that may be subject to use.

Every year the Evanston Voluntary Fire Department would sponsor a fireman's ball to raise money for their department. Most of the money raised was used for their personal fire equipment and clothing. But that year the city purchased a new firetruck and a chief's car. The City of Evanston had always been anxious to help the department in any way they could. Both the mayor and city council had always been very proud of the department, mainly because they were all volunteers and were more than willing to put their lives on the line to help others. They also did a terrific job in responding to fires and other emergencies outside the Evanston area. They assisted in emergency calls as far away as Woodruff and Randolph, Utah when needed.

Also, that year Police Officer Sherman Rollins received an award for Distinguished and Meritorious Service by the Evanston Lion's Club. The honor was presented by the president of the Stockgrowers Bank, Vern Smith. The honor was presented to Officer Rollins for valor, fast thinking and quick action in thwarting a possible bank robbery by wounding and capturing the suspect in action. It was an award well deserved.

This was about the time when prices started increasing. Inflation had hit and prices were rising fast. It seemed like everything was on the up rise. No more nickel coffee, or 30 cent per gallon gasoline, and no more 3 cent postage stamps. Coffee was on the rise big time and so were many other commodities. Postage stamps had been increased to 8 cents for regular mail and gasoline was up to 50 cents a gallon. Prices were rising fast, but wages were lagging way behind causing difficult times for many families.

The City of Evanston's economy was starting to be a concern as well. One big reason was because of all the rumors floating around about the railroad and the changes they were supposedly making. All this talk was slowly becoming a reality and it was starting to worry the entire community. The rise in prices wasn't the only thing we were concerned about. The city had started talking about raising sewer and water rates, but we held off for a while longer. But at this time, the railroad discontinued all regular passenger train service and that had us worried.

All railroad passenger service had been discontinued throughout the State of Wyoming, but because of pressure from Governor Hathaway and Wyoming's Congressional members, the railroad and the U.S. Government tested a system called the Railpak Network through the southern route of Wyoming. After a short tryout, though, they completely dropped it. Wyoming was now the only state in the nation without any passenger rail service.

Later on, the system called Railpak was changed to a new system called Amtrak, and Southern Wyoming was once again included with passenger service, thanks once again to our Governor and our Congressional group. Amtrak would run from Chicago to Denver, then through Wyoming to Ogden, Utah and from there to the west coast, but it didn't last long.

That spring Albert Pilch, member of the state Recreation Commission, introduced a plan to establish a state park on land owned by the state just east of Evanston. There would be 1,400 acres with the Bear River running through it. The mayor and council all thought it was a great idea and would be a big asset to the community. I was very excited about it and everyone gave their support.

But at that time a lot of the golf advocates, myself included, were hoping to someday move the golf course to the location now being considered by Pilch for a state park. After hearing his plan and thinking about it, a lot of us decided that his idea was a good one. It would be a number of years down the road before the park became a reality, but Pilch and some of those in government never gave up on the idea. Evanston would eventually have that state park.

Also that year, the Wyoming Highway Department announced that they were going to do a traffic study for Evanston and requested some assistance from the city. So Mayor Burns appointed an advisory board to assist them. His appointments were Sam Hart, John Proffit and Blaine Sanders. It appeared that our biggest concern would be the underpass, as it was the only way to get from one side of town to the other unless you went out on the freeway.

In other business that year, we added another hangar and workshop building at the airport, and, in addition to what we had already purchased for the fire department, we bought a new diesel engine firetruck. We also worked on animal control and noise ordinances. We received another matching fund grant from the state in the amount of $48,000 to enlarge the golf course. We also had complaints about some people neglecting their horses, especially along the County Road area.

Eugene Martin, as a local businessman, came to the council meeting to discuss concerns about all the vacant buildings in town. This was something we all agreed was making our community look bad. After some discussion Council Members Bill George and Ron Davis volunteered to look into the problem.

Marvin Bollschweiler, Water Commissioner of Uinta County, met with the city council and suggested that the city register all water rights of the golf course properties into the city water system. He said this should be done even if the city was just leasing the property. Mayor Burns thanked Mr. Bollschweiler for the information and directed City Attorney Vehar to look into the matter.

Although the year was busy and moving along pretty well, except for the poor economy, in late September Evanston was hit with one hell of a bombshell. Mr. John C. Kenefick, president of the Union Pacific Railroad, announced that the Evanston Union Pacific Reclamation Plant would be completely shut down and moved to Cheyenne along with some employees. This was a shock for Evanston, especially the employees. We were expecting some changes, but nothing like this. The Uinta County Herald headlines on January 6, 1972 read: U.P. RECLAMATION PLANT CLOSED FRIDAY, DECEMBER 31.

Mayor Burns immediately called for a special council meeting and after a considerable amount of discussion he stated that he would write to Governor Stan Hathaway and to our Congressional delegation, Senators Gale McGee and Clifford Hansen and Representative Teno Roncallio to seek whatever assistance they could give us to be able to retain the plant in Evanston.

Mayor Burns also contacted Ed Sencabaugh, Special Representative to President Kenefick. Sencabaugh lived in Cheyenne and had been a past president of the Wyoming Jaycees at the time Burns had also been very active in that organization. During the time they spent together as Jaycee members, they had become good friends. After Burns explained how the plant closing was going to affect the city, Sencabaugh stated that he would talk to Kenefick and get back to Burns.

At this time there were over 300 employees working at the plant. Therefore, by shutting the plant down completely, Evanston could lose 300 families. Nothing could hurt the economy more. Evanston's economy was already on the decline because of the freeway and other changes that had affected the economy in the past. This had an enormous effect on the folks in Evanston, especially the businesspeople, who were wondering what was going to happen next.

Another bombshell came in November: Evanston was hit with a winter storm that brought blinding blizzards, very high winds and 18 inches of snow. Approximately one hundred trucks were stalled, plus hundreds of tourists and highway travelers were stranded in Evanston. Roads were closed both ways and Evanston was loaded down with an excessive amount of visitors. The community was so overrun with people that they had to use the Wyoming State Hospital and the Wyoming National Guard Armory for additional places for people to stay. There were approximately 2,000 people stranded, and Evanston did everything they could to comfort them.

At the December council meeting, because of all the problems facing Evanston, there was a large attendance of concerned citizens. Most had to stand because the meeting room was so small. The economy was the main topic, but we also talked about what the Greater Evanston Development Company could do and what could be done about our transportation and railroad problems.

As president of the G.E.D.C., I told them that our first priority was to work on bringing new industry to Evanston. We would push the new S.B.A. 502 program as hard and fast as we could, and that we would not be standing still. Mayor Burns assured the citizens that we were doing everything we could to keep some of the Union Pacific here, and that we would create an advisory board to look into our transportation problem. One of the main issues that came up con-cerning transportation was the relocation of Highway 89 (also known as County Road).

We decided to do a transportation study. The study board was formed with about 12 people volunteering to serve. The board in-cluded Mayor Burns, Councilman Christensen, Uinta County Com-missioner, L. S. (Ren) South and several businessmen from all over town.

Yep, 1971 was some kind of a year, but what was ahead of us was also going to be affecting Evanston in a big way with still more changes.

CHAPTER 6

972....It was now 1972, an election year, the presidential election year. Three members of the city council would be up for re-election. I wasn't sure they would all run again for re-election because Evanston was facing a ton of problems.

Closing down the reclamation plant on December 31, 1971 was a terrible thing to happen to the employees during the Christmas holidays and on New Year's Eve day, and what an appalling economic break for the community! This really put the city in a depressed situation, but there wasn't too much we could do about it except keep going and continue our efforts to better the economy.

The first meeting of the month, on January 7th, was a short one. There wasn't much talk about the shutdown; there wasn't much to say. After the mayor made his appointments we heard, once again, from the only citizen present, Marvin Bollschweiler. He was there to remind us again to convey all water rights in the city to municipal use. He stated that this could be very important to the city. Mayor Burns assured him that Mr. Vehar, the city attorney, was working on it. The mayor thanked Mr. Bollschweiler for keeping us informed.

On January 10th, the mayor called for a special meeting to assign the different departments to the council. He appointed Arnold Christensen to oversee garbage and sanitation, William "Bill" George to streets and alleys, Melvin Baldwin to the cemetery, and Royce Bills to the airport. The mayor assigned himself to oversee the police department, and my assignment was once again Parks and Recreation, and again the Planning and Zoning Board (thank you, Mayor!).

I was glad that he kept me in recreation, because right from the start my dream was to see the City of Evanston have a big recreation center someday, with a swimming pool and facilities that would be available to citizens of all ages. It was my goal to see this completed, but it was another ten or so years away before it actually happened.

During this meeting we also discussed the garbage problem that had arisen due to a new ruling that the government came out with about burning at our city dumps: There were to be no more open dumps and no more burning. We discussed the possibility of a land-fill, but the location was going to be a problem. We also discussed the dog problem again. We seemed to be getting more and more complaints all the time. The mayor asked the council members to come up with some ideas.

That January, we received the last of the federal grant funds for Anderson Park from the Wyoming Recreation Commission, in the amount of $4,873.46.

During our February meeting, appointments to the Planning and Zoning Board and the Board of Adjustments were made. I was the councilman assigned to P & Z, and it was up to me to give recommendations, so I recommended Edward Jones, Blaine Sanders and Merlyn Kunz for the 1-year term, Lamar Day, Vern Smith and Charles Albrecht for 2 years, and Duane Shupe, James Cronister and Leland S. Sims for 3 years. Three-year appointments to the Board of Adjustments included me as chairman, and Duane Shupe, Lamar Day, Charles Albrecht and Leland S. Sims. All were approved by the council.

Also, that month the Evanston Quarterback Club donated a to-boggan to the Eagle Rock Ski Patrol, the city purchased a new police patrol car, and we set the dates of the four special days that the liquor dealers could stay open continuously.

On March 3, Evanston had the honor of holding the Wyoming State Ski Meet. This was an indication that our own ski hill, Eagle Rock, was doing great and a lot of our kids were learning to ski here and participating in the school's program. During this meeting we also discussed the water problems that this winter caused. Because of the frost going so deep into the ground it caused a lot of freeze-ups in the water lines. We knew that come spring, we would be looking at the possibility of lowering some of those lines.

About this time the Union Pacific Railroad Company offered to give to the City of Evanston the old coal burning switch engine that we called "the goat." This engine was the yard engine that they used for switching cars around the Union Pacific yard. When I was a fireman on the railroad back in 1953 and 1954 I fired that engine. If I remember right, I had to fire it by hand most of the time. The two engineers that I remember working with were Heber Warburton and Jake Jacobsen. They are long since gone now, but I thought they both were a couple of great guys to work with.

The U.P. gave the engine to the city, but there were two big problems. First, where were we going to put it, and second, how were we going to get it there? The county, at that time, had a gazebo located on the Main Street side of an old county building. The county commissioners said they would tear the gazebo down and the city could locate the engine in its place. The commissioners indicated that they had been planning to do away with the gazebo for a long time. The big question now was, how were we going to get it there?

A lot of citizens were against tearing down the gazebo. Some would go there to relax and enjoy themselves and kids would go there to play, but I guess it was a problem for the county to keep it maintained. What I remember about the gazebo was that once a week the local band would play in front of a crowd of locals and amuse them with their music. Some of the musicians that I recall were Bob Skyles, George Stevenson, Bob "Tobe" Tueller and Fred Kallas. A lot of the locals looked forward to it every week.

The U.P.R.R. said they would get the engine moved to the location as soon as the gazebo was gone. They laid track down on the streets from the yard to the courthouse location and drove the engine to the location. I don't recall which direction they went, but I do know they got it there and in place, and it stayed there until 1983, at which time it was carried by truck to its present location at Railroad Park. While it was at the County Courthouse yards, the local kids got the chance to play on the engine and find out first-hand what one looked like.

Other business we took care of that year was: we raised swimming rates at the city swimming pool; we installed a new fence along the east border of the cemetery at the request of the Painter Ranch because their cattle kept wandering into the cemetery grounds and causing damage; and we passed into law a new and very lengthy animal control ordinance. That year, with a shortage of water, we set the necessary restrictions on water irrigation. We used the odd and even house number system again. And we received another grant in the amount of $16,951.43 for the Eagle Rock Ski project. The grant came from the Federal Land and Conservation Fund, but was presented through the Wyoming Recreation Commission by board member Albert Pilch.

Mayor Burns called for a special meeting on June 23, 1972 to pass on the third and final reading of the ordinance allowing the city to officially form an airport board. We also discussed some amendments to the garbage ordinance and the possibility of raising rates. The solid waste department was under the supervision of Verdon Moore, who had been with the city for many years. Moore had been driving the garbage truck for quite some time while two employees would ride on the tailgate ready to stop at every house and business to dump the garbage cans into the dumping bin of the truck.

At that time every house and every business used 55-gallon drums for garbage, and some businesses had two, three or maybe even four of those drums. We couldn't keep employees on the garbage truck very long, mainly because the drums were so heavy that it always took two men to dump a drum into the truck bin. The drums generally were pretty full and sometimes, in the winter months, they may have been half full of ice because they had no lids and the snow or rain would get in the drum and freeze, creating heavy ice at the bottom of the drum. Almost all of those that worked on the garbage truck ended up with bad backs from lifting those drums. At that time the city had no insurance program for them, but no one stayed in that department very long. Moore had a hard time keeping the same men for any length of time. They would either quit or wiggle their way into another department.

At that time, the city public works shop was located on Front Street between 11th (Harrison Drive) and 12th Street. It was located across the street from where the Fire Department building is at present. The old Condos home was located on the northwest side of the shop, and the Sim hotel was located on the other side. The shop wasn't very big; therefore we were unable to keep any vehicles inside, only small equipment, and the outside area where we parked the large equipment wasn't very large either. In the wintertime, the drivers would start up their vehicles and let them warm up before putting them to work. It was pretty inconvenient for the employees.

We didn't have a lot of equipment at first, but when we did start getting additional equipment we were tight on space and didn't have room for the garbage truck any longer, so we told Moore that he would have to leave his truck at the dumps. He didn't like that, but he went along with it anyway. The dumps at that time were located just off the present East Service Road on the northwest side. The city dump was an open area, used by the public as well as the city. It was continuously burning, which was illegal according to the federal government, so we had to find another location for a landfill. We were being pushed by the feds pretty hard, but it would still be a while before we located a new area.

During that same meeting, one of the amendments brought up was to change the size of the drums. We ended up going with the 33 and 35 gallon cans with covers because one man could handle a can, but we kept two men on the tailgate because they could work much faster. The city furnished cans to all houses and businesses, but we raised the garbage pickup rate to offset the cost of the cans. This made it a lot easier on the crew and we were able to keep the employees longer. However, it still wasn't a very pleasant job.

After passing the ordinance pertaining to the airport the mayor made these new appointments to the board: Jack Kreider, 1 year; Don Barnard, 2 years; Duane Shupe, 3 years; Roy Turner, 4 years; and Dr. S. L. Ekins, 5 years. The ordinance made this board official and it would be assisting the mayor in locating a new site for the airport.

The opening date for filing for office for the upcoming election was in June. Those who filed for city council were Arnold Christensen in Ward 1, who filed for re-election with Jon Lunsford and Russell "Bub"

Albrecht opposing him; Mel Baldwin who filed for re-election in Ward 2 with Don Welling opposing him; and Walter "Sterk" Aanerud and Roger Fife filed for Ward 3. Bill George did not run again.

That summer, the Greater Evanston Development Company had their annual meeting with the election of officers at the new fire hall. The election was held and they voted me in as president again, Ed Stephens as Vice President, Robert "Bob" Duncan as Secretary and Blaine Sanders as Treasurer. Others elected as Directors were Herschel Goldsby, Mayor Bob Burns and Roger Fife.

Mayor Burns, returning from his trip to Omaha with Ed Sencabaugh, announced that after meeting with the officials of the Union Pacific Railroad, Mr. Kenefick, president of U.P., agreed to donate to the City of Evanston the 26 acres of property where the reclamation plant, machine shop, and other buildings were located, plus whatever equipment was left. Mr. Kenefick said that the official transfer of the deed would be completed sometime later that year. He also said that this should help Evanston in their efforts in trying to bring new industry to the area.

During the meeting, Mayor Burns asked the Greater Evanston Development Company to come up with an industrial plan for the reclamation plant area. He said we needed something to show to potential companies that may be interested in relocating to Evanston. He also announced that he had been talking to the Wyoming Economic Commission on some items of interest. He told us that through the state board, he had heard that there was a railway car company called the Texas Rail Car Company, near Abilene, Texas that might be interested in setting up another repair shop in Evanston. The word was that they might be interested in leasing the roundhouse property from the city. After hearing this, Mayor Burns immediately got in touch with the Texas Railway Car Company and invited them to Evanston for an on-site meeting with city officials and members of the development company.

The meeting was set up for the latter part of July with officials from Texas. Colonel Oliver Shiflet, president of the Texas Railway Car Company and Joe Williams, Vice President, attended the meeting.

Col. Shiflet showed a lot of interest, but he said that he would need help from the Evanston development group to obtain a loan through the S.B.A. 502 program. The development company assured him that they would do everything possible to help get him started. This was a great opportunity to help get the economy going and we were going to try very hard to make this happen, but it would be another year or so before it became a reality.

In August, the Uinta County Commissioners announced that the county was anticipating buying the old Methodist Church building, located on the corner of 10th Street and Center Street, to be used for the Uinta County Senior Citizens group. I believe at that time Louise Karn was the director. The senior citizens of Uinta County would now have a decent center to enjoy.

After several hearings and special meetings, the City of Evanston's budget for the fiscal year of 1972 and 1973 was heard by the public again and passed by the council during the regular meeting of August 2, 1972. The total amount passed was just over $440,000.00. Not much of a budget, but you had to stay within the amount of your anticipated revenues. We always hoped that the revenues received would exceed the amount of the budget, because if it didn't we would be looking at cuts throughout the year.

Every indication showed that Evanston was declining in pop-ulation. The school district came out with an enrollment of 1,103 students for the 1972 school year. They said that it would be a drop of about 55 students. It was reasonable to assume that if the school was losing population, the city must also be losing.

The winners of the primary election for city councilman who would run in the general election were Lunsford and Albrecht for Ward 1, Baldwin and Welling for Ward 2, and Fife and Aanerud for Ward 3. The general election would be in November.

In September, it was announced that Frank Woolley received through the G.E.D.C. and S.B.A. a loan in the amount of $514,000.00 to add 50 more motel rooms to the Ramada Inn, which already had 47 rooms. The bank would loan the estimated balance of the project, which was 90% of the total.

A luncheon was held at the Jolly Roger Restaurant on October 21, 1972 where the Union Pacific Railroad presented a deed to the City of Evanston for the 26 acres of prime industrial land, which included the roundhouse, the machine shop, the woodshop and other valuable buildings, including dozens of major items of equipment and other miscellaneous items. It did not include the power plant, because it was sitting on the railroad right-of-way, which was not part of the property deeded to the city. However, it did include the equipment in it. The entire area was heated from that plant so they had to keep it in operation until changes could be made. The Uinta County Herald headline for their October 26th issue read, "Union Pacific Presented Deed."

Mr. Scotty Durrant, General Manager of the U.P.R.R. made the presentation to Evanston Mayor Bob Burns. Others present were U.P. officials, Wyoming dignitaries, city officials and members of the G.E.D.C. Mr. Durrant complimented Mayor Burns and other officials on their effort in getting the U.P. to give the city the reclamation plant and the 26 acres. *We are pleased*, he said, *to have the opportunity to come to the front to help rebuild the economy of Evanston.* Mayor Burns thanked Mr. Durrant and told him, having this property and the facilities on it we can now pursue our plans for new industry to come to Evanston.

In October, 1972 Evanston lost one of its finest citizens. Edward Jones, Evanston's fire chief, passed away. Jones was an employee of the Union Pacific Railroad, I believe in Omaha, when he was transferred to Evanston with others to play on the U.P.R.R. baseball team that was competing in a league against other cities throughout the western area back in the 1930s and '40s, until World War II was declared. Jones was an exceptionally good ball player. He had been fire chief for several years and had been a great supporter of Evanston.

During the November 3rd meeting, after the death of Ed Jones, Mayor Bob Burns appointed Gerald Cazin as Fire Chief. Cazin had been Assistant Chief to Jones. The mayor also appointed Jack O'Brian as Assistant Chief. Both were well experienced.

At this meeting some of the members of the G.E.D.C. board met with the city to report on the industrial plan that they had been working on concerning the property that the U.P. gave the city. They helped assure the mayor and city council that we were working hard to get things done. Those that showed up were Sanders, Stephens and Goldsby.

The general election was over and President Richard Nixon won his second term. The city councilmen that got elected were Jon Lunsford, Ward 1; Mel Baldwin, Ward 2; and Roger Fife, Ward 3. We now would have a couple new heads on the council come January.

During our regular meeting, December 4, 1972 Bert Phillips was appointed as City Engineer after John Proffit resigned and left Evanston because of the economy. There apparently was no longer enough work in the area for Proffit Engineering, so they shut down and John and his family and part of his crew left Evanston, but they all returned a few years later when the economy got better.

At the meeting, Mayor Burns directed Phillips to look into creating some kind of bypass to help eliminate the groundwater problem. During heavy rain storms and cloud bursts, our catch basins would back up and cause flooding on some of the streets.

A special meeting was called on December 12th to discuss the Greater Evanston Development Company's part in getting the Texas Railway Car Company to come to Evanston. There was a motion made to lease the property, at no rate, to the development company and give them control of planning and developing the 26 acres of the railroad property. The idea was that the development company would receive the lease monies from whoever leased the property so that they could gain enough funds to be able to assist other types of business in applying for the S.B.A. 502 loans. The equipment and all loose items would be under the control of the development company. The motion was made and passed, all voting in favor. This was another big job for me to take care of and worry about, but I would have a lot of help. I had a good bunch in the company to help me out. We retained Lee Harris as our attorney to assist us in all our legal problems.

Other business brought up was the mayor's request to hire Frank Pollard, a part time retiree, to assist the police department to act as the night patrolman during the holiday season, because we had been having a number of burglaries and robberies lately. Motion was made and passed, all voting in favor.

Also, a resolution was passed on the two hour parking limit in downtown Evanston. In addition to the meters, tires would be chalked and violators of the two hour rule would be ticketed. We hoped that this would help with the downtown parking problem, especially by stopping the merchants and professional people from parking in front of the stores all day. Sometimes, instead of parking in front of their own store or office, they would park somewhere down the street, often in front of other businesses. We had the meters, but people would either just ignore them or, every once in a while, go out to the meter and add another coin. They apparently knew about when the meters would be checked, but we still chalked the tires.

CHAPTER 7

1973....At the end of the year on December 21, 1972 a fire totally destroyed the chair lift at the Eagle Rock Ski Area. During the investigation it was determined to be arson. Someone deliberately intended to destroy Eagle Rock. The damage was estimated at about $20,000. Various clubs and organizations in Evanston put out a reward of $1,000 for any information leading to the arrest of the arsonist. Eagle Rock was shut down for the rest of that season.

During the January, 1973 the city received another grant in the amount of $10,439 from the Federal Land and Conservation Fund through the Wyoming Recreation Commission. The funds were to be used for the golf course water system.

After swearing in the new council members and Baldwin at our regular meeting, Mayor Burns made his council assignments. They were as follows: Streets and alleys were assigned to Lunsford and Davis, water to Fife and me, sanitary (garbage) to Bills and Lunsford, Parks and Recreation to Fife and me, Airport to Bills and Mayor Burns, cemetery to Baldwin and Bills, Planning and Zoning to Baldwin and Fife, Animal Control to Davis and Mayor Burns, and police to Mayor Burns. Doubling up on the various departments was new to the council. Mayor Burns's idea was that putting more than one councilman in charge of a department would give the council members an opportunity to work more closely together and understand department problems better. It did turn out to be workable and seemed to bring council members closer together.

The Greater Evanston Development Company board reported that plans were progressing to get the new railway car company to become a reality. It was reported that Lamar Day of the Utah Power and Light Company would be going to Texas to talk to Colonel Shiflet about what power would be needed at the plant. His visit was also to show Shiflet and his partners that the city was very serious in soliciting them to set up a plant in Evanston.

When the Union Pacific deeded the 26 acres to the City of Evanston, the city leased an acre of the property on the corner of Front Street and 12th Street to Time-DC, a trucking company out of Denver, Colorado that had recently moved their dispatch office to Evanston. They set up a temporary office building on the property they were leasing (where the present city hall and parking lot is located). They used the property not only for their office, but also for parking their trucks. When Time-DC came to Evanston they weren't intending on making it permanent, but they did lease the property for several years. When they pulled the office out, several of their drivers remained in Evanston with their families and made their homes here. Some of the drivers I recall were Bob Dean, Otto Ledgerwood, Ed Bowie, Jim Reeves, Lenz Cheatham and Tom Van-Syoc, the dispatcher. Also, one of the drivers, Bob Moore, made his home in Bridger Valley.

In addition, Montgomery Ward's trucks were being dispatched out of Evanston with a couple of drivers living here. One of those drivers, Jim Cronister, stayed in Evanston with his family after Ward's trucking left. He stayed here and started his own business and raised his family in Evanston.

Having these trucking companies in Evanston did help the economy somewhat during a period when the town was looking pretty bleak. After the railroad left, things didn't look too good. All we could do was keep working towards trying to better the community, and hope for a big break in improving the economy.

Other business during that winter included applying for federal funds to assist us in finding a location for the new landfill. We put a moratorium on allowing house trailers and mobile homes until a study could be completed, and we began the preliminary action towards the adoption of the National Codes such as building codes and fire prevention codes. Jerry Cazin, the fire chief, passed out copies of the national fire codes, and, by unanimous vote, Benny Goodwin was appointed as Assistant Fire Chief in place of Jack O'Brian, who had resigned because of health problems.

During this time we had a request from the Uinta County Senior Citizens to come up with Pioneer Parking Permits for those of 65 years of age and older to have free parking. We also discussed another Improvement District to upgrade more of the streets that were still gravel. The Improvement District would include paving, curb and gutter. Both of these issues were tabled for a later meeting.

Within the 26 acres of property that the Union Pacific Railroad deeded to the City of Evanston, there was a house that was located up on the hill just off Main Street and across from the roundhouse, where the family of Mr. Clarence Palmer, a railroad worker, had lived for years, but had since moved away. At this time the property was vacant. A son, Jerry Palmer, and other members of the Palmer family met with the mayor and city council to request to purchase the house and the small lot it sat on. The Palmers indicated that they had lived there during their childhood and felt that there was some sentimental value to them to be able to purchase the property. After a considerable amount of discussion it was moved and seconded by the council to sell the property to them at the appraised value. All voted in favor.

In April, we received another small grant in the amount of $5,400 for the golf course, and on May 4, 1973 Mayor Burns was appointed to the Wyoming Aeronautics Commission by Governor Hathaway for a six-year term.

Also in April, we got word that Frank A. Woolley had died on Sunday, April 22, 1973. It was reported that he had been on a scaffold high up on a building that he was constructing at his shopping center in Ogden when he fell off, and had died of his injuries at the hospital. This was very sad news for Evanston. Woolley had been one of Evanston's most prominent businessmen and had big plans for projects in that would have helped the city's economy a lot. He was also the person who brought the S.B.A. 502 Program to us and helped form the Greater Evanston Development Company. He was a great guy and a major part of Evanston. He left quite a legacy.

That spring the Stockgrowers Bank, located at 928 Main Street, had purchased the Lincoln Service, which had the Chevrolet, Buick and Oldsmobile dealerships. They were located on the corner of 9th Street and Main Street. The bank purchased to build a larger bank building. The bank demolished all existing buildings and built an entirely new structure. The dealership purchased some property on the east end of Evanston and relocated their business there. About that same time Mayor Burns and his wife Connie, along with my wife Sandy and me, plus Harry Lee Harris and his wife June traveled to Texas to meet with Colonel Shiflet and his partners. I went as president representing the G.E.D.C., and Lee Harris went as G.E.D.C.'s attorney. The mayor, of course, went to represent the city. Our sole purpose for going there was to check out the Texas Railway Car Company and to try to come up with a deal for the colonel and his associates to open up a car company facility in Evanston.

We flew into Dallas, where Colonel Shiflet picked us up and drove us to Abilene, where he lived, and where we met with him and his group to talk about their move to Evanston. They all sounded very serious and so the colonel and his wife, Valora, drove us over to Ranger, Texas where their railway car plant was. Ranger was just off Interstate 20 about 50 miles east of Abilene. We got the opportunity to tour their plant. We were all very impressed with the entire setup.

In meeting with the Texas group, we were pretty encouraged with how the meeting went and were hoping for a definite decision on their part at that time, but I guess we were expecting too much too soon. They claimed that it was a bit too early to make any commitment right then. They said that they needed more time to do some more checking into it before they made any commitments, but they said that they were very interested and would probably let us know within the next few weeks.

While we were in Texas, Connie called home to see how her father was, because he had been ill, only to find out that he had died while she was gone. This cut the Burns's visit short and they immediately returned to the airport in Dallas and got an emergency flight for home, but our flight wasn't due to leave until the next day, so we had some time to burn in Dallas. We rented a car and went to downtown Dallas to spend some time and visit the memorial where President John F. Kennedy was murdered. While there, Sandy and June spotted a Nieman-Marcus store, which had the reputation of being a very expensive women's dress shop. So they thought they might just go check it out. It was pretty exciting for Sandy, because she had never been in a store like that before. I didn't know whether June had experienced it or not, but when they came out I don't believe June had purchased anything, but Sandy had a Nieman-Marcus shopping bag with nothing in it and I asked her why she had it. She told me that the bag cost her $5.00 and it was the only thing in the whole store that she could afford, and that she wanted the bag to show people that she had been there. We all just laughed.

Our economy was getting pretty bleak at the time, when we got hit with another big surprise from the railroad. They moved the locomotive engineer and firemen's dispatch office completely out of Evanston, where it had been for years. They moved it to Ogden, Utah. Most of the engine crews lived in Evanston at that time, but now almost all of them relocated their families to the Ogden area. Evanston lost several dozen more families. Things were looking pretty bad for the community, and the city had only one goal: to improve the economy. It was amazing the way most businesses stayed open. Some moved around to different locations, because of the freeway and such, but they still stuck around.

That spring we worked on the Comprehensive Plan with the planning board, we talked about restoring the chair lift at Eagle Rock and we worked on updating the zoning ordinance. More trees were planted at the golf course. The course was only a nine-hole course, but it was looking really good. Everyone seemed to appreciate what had been done since the city took it over.

About this time our Chief of Police, Charles "Chuck" Overy, had presented the mayor with his resignation. He said he was leaving Evanston and going to Kemmerer to live for a while. So at the next meeting the mayor appointed Sherman Rollins as Acting Chief of Police until we had time to advertise for the position. Rollins didn't particularly want it, but said he would do it until we found someone else.

That spring, we hired Ray Crandall of the Intermountain Ski Lift Company to restore and repair the damage to the chair lift that was caused by the fire we had in December at Eagle Rock. Crandall had been the person that installed it initially, and he assured us that it would be completed by the next season, but it wasn't. It took a little longer than anticipated and the hill didn't open back up again until after the first of the year, 1974.

Other business taken up during that spring was that the city sold a piece of city-owned property at the eastern end of Center Street to the high bidder, Jay Dee Kindler; we had more sewer problems; and we set June 1st as the date for the public hearing concerning the new planning and zoning ordinance. This ordinance was one of the most lengthy and long-winded ordinances that had been introduced for adoption during the time I had been a member of the city council. By law we had to publish the ordinance in its entirety for the public's interest, which took up almost half of that issue of the Uinta County Herald. Like all ordinances, it was very costly to have published.

A delegation from the city employees approached the council requesting a 25% increase in pay. The mayor and council agreed that they certainly deserved an increase, but we told them that we would have to wait and see what the budget looked like. The employees hadn't had an increase in pay for quite some time, and with inflation and the cost of living rising like it was, there was no way we could refuse them some kind of raise. A sizeable increase was added to the next fiscal budget. It wasn't quite as much as they asked for, but it made the employees feel good, even though it still wasn't keeping up with inflation and the cost of living.

During the regular council meeting on May 2nd, Mayor Burns read the following letter dated on April 30, 1973 from Vern J. Smith, Chairman of the Evanston Planning and Zoning Commission:

To the Mayor and City Council
City of Evanston

Gentlemen:
As your duly appointed Planning and Zoning Commission and at your direction we have been working on the updating and overall revision of the Comprehensive Plan for the City of Evanston.

In line with these directions we have been preparing a new Zoning Ordinance, which will be applicable and useful to the City of Evanston.

At our meeting held on the 30th of April 1973 at 8:00 P.M. in the City Council chambers, it was moved by Mr. Duane Shupe and seconded by Mr. LaMar Day that the Evanston City Planning and Zoning Commission certify to the City Council the proposed ordinance. The motion was adopted by all voting "aye," a legal quorum being in attendance.

We do so certify said ordinance to your body with our whole-hearted recommendation that it be adopted speedily for the betterment of our community.

V. J. Smith – Chairman
Evanston City Planning and Zoning Commission

Mr. Smith then pointed out that the old zoning ordinance had served its purpose, and they had distributed copies of the commission's new proposed ordinance to the mayor and each council member. He also presented a map showing the changes and had it explained to the council by Mr. J. Newell Sorenson, County Planner.

Mayor Burns thanked Mr. Smith and the commission for all their hard work and interest and stated that, *if the required publication of the ordinance can be met, a tentative date of June 1st will be set for the necessary public hearing concerning the proposed ordinance.*

As advertised, on June 1st the public hearing was held concerning the new planning and zoning ordinance, but there was such a large crowd that we had to move the meeting from the small city council room to the new fire hall. Although the City of Evanston was in a depression at this time and losing population, there still seemed to be a tremendous amount of interest in the ordinance.

The new proposed ordinance was presented to the public and explained to them by Mr. Smith and Mr. Sorenson. A general discussion followed, and all questions were answered, resulting in some changes and deletions being recommended. It was decided that some of these recommendations would be incorporated into the proposed ordinance and the ordinance would be presented to the mayor and city council to act on at their next regular city council meeting on June 4th.

During the meeting of June 4th, Ordinance 286, the new proposed planning and zoning ordinance, was introduced by me and moved and seconded for passage on first reading. Mayor Burns then opened the floor up for discussion. The meeting lasted for hours with a lot of discussion on this particular issue, but most of those present were more concerned with how it was going to affect them rather than how it would help the city in the future.

Motion was made and seconded for passage on first reading, with five councilmen voting aye and one absent. The motion passed on first reading. Mayor Burns then assured the public that this ordinance would go through two more readings before being passed on final reading, and that anyone would be welcome to be present at those meetings for more discussion if necessary.

Therefore, a few meetings and a few amendments later, the P & Z ordinance was finally passed for adoption on second reading with all voting in favor, and on third and final reading with all voting in favor.

At our regular meeting of June 4th the Catholic Church requested that the city take over the maintenance of the Catholic cemetery because of their lack of funds to take care of it. The mayor explained to them that if the city did take it over that it would no longer be for just their church members—that it would be open for the general public, plus what funds they were holding for the cemetery would need to be turned over to the city. The delegation from the church that was present at the meeting stated that they had a discussion with the members and they were very much aware of what the city would require and had no problems with it. After more discussion, a motion was made and seconded with all voting in favor. Mayor Burns directed Mr. Vehar, City Attorney to take care of whatever legal work had to be done.

Mayor Burns announced that he had been elected as president of the Wyoming Association of Municipalities (W. A. M.) for the next year. Burns had been vice president the previous year and was elected as president at the recent annual meeting in June for the coming year.

At our regular meeting in June we also talked about advertising for a new Chief of Police. Also, we started looking over the new 1973-1974 budget, hoping it would meet all necessary funding. Public hearing for the new fiscal year budget was advertised to be presented at our regular meeting on July 3rd.

The July meeting was a long and drawn-out meeting because of all the discussion of the budget, the Improvement District concerning certain streets, a nuisance ordinance that came up and was discussed, and the police report on the many break-ins and burglaries occurring at that time. It was a busy evening.

The fiscal year budget for 1973-1974 was adopted and passed in an amount exceeding $472,000, Evanston's highest budget up until that time. Although the economy was down, we were able to give a well deserved increase in pay to the employees. Of course it wasn't what they asked for, but they all seemed to be well satisfied.

In September, Edgar Vinneman, Jr., Mayor of Evanston, Illinois and his family had called Mayor Burns and told him that they were coming to Evanston to visit for few days, because of the two cities having the same name. Mayor Burns and wife Connie entertained the Vinneman family during their stay. Vinneman was under the misunderstanding that Evanston, Wyoming was named after the same person that Evanston, Illinois was named after, but that error was corrected. Evanston, Illinois was named after a railroad civil engineer named John Evans that worked on the railroad while it was under construction in Colorado. Our smaller city was named after James Evans, a young railroad surveyor and engineer, who worked on the construction of the Union Pacific Railroad through Wyoming.

The two mayors seemed to enjoy comparing and discussing their problems, some of which were similar, but Evanston, Illinois had a population of about 80,000 people at that time, and our community had just over 4,000. I'm sure Mayor Vinneman had much larger problems than we did, but the mayor and his family appeared to enjoy their visit and left thanking us for our hospitality and wished us well.

Also about this time, a local group of businessmen had purchased a section of property from the state of Wyoming south of the freeway. Some of those involved were my brother Bob along with Cloey Wall, Ed Stevens, Dub Mills, Harvey Johnston and several others. They originally purchased the property to construct an establishment for horse racing, since Wyoming had approved parimutuel betting, and they thought that would be an excellent location for it. The group thought that with Utah right next door that horse racing would go over great for Evanston and help the economy a lot.

At our regular meeting on September 5th, the group approached the city council about annexing the property. Their representative, Cloey Wall, explained to the council what their plans were and that they wished to have part of the property annexed. After some discussion, Mayor Burns explained to them that they needed to make an application and go through the proper steps. He also told them that he liked the idea of the racetrack, and that it would help tremendously in improving our economy, and at this time the economy needed a good boost. However, the racetrack idea never happened. A few years later, the group sold the property to a real estate broker named Doyle Child, owner of Hoback Realty of Afton, Wyoming. Hoback then subdivided the property, with the first subdivision being called Uinta Meadows, not too long after they purchased the property.

During that meeting we also lifted the moratorium on building, although we were still having sewer problems. We were seeking a new location and some funding for a new sewer plant, but that did not come about for several more years. Also, Mayor Burns announced that the Governor of Wyoming had formed a Planning Committee on Criminal Administration, and that the governor had appointed me to serve on the committee to represent towns and cities, and Gene Taylor, County Commissioner, to represent counties. This gave me another job to think about, but I was grateful for the appointment.

The Uinta County Herald came out with an article in their September 27th issue commemorating the 16-year anniversary since the Evanston's Non-profit TV Corporation's UHF television was established. It had served Evanston with good television for years, but in the October 4th issue of the Herald, it was announced that Mayor Bob Burns, who had owned the Western Auto store for years, was in process of bringing cable television to Evanston, which would have an effect on the non-profit company and eventually put them out of business.

Mayor Burns purchased Western Auto from Frank Emerson several years ago and went into the business of selling and repairing televisions while he had the store. Burns had been friends through the Wyoming Jaycees with Jerry Corolla of Green River, Wyoming whose family owned the Sweetwater Cable Television Company in Sweetwater County. Corolla, through advice and assistance, helped Burns get cable started in the Evanston area, but Burns first had to obtain a utility franchise with the City of Evanston to utilize the streets and alleys.

Mayor Burns called for a special meeting on September 21st to discuss the parking meter problems between 11th and 12th Streets on Main, plus the dog problems that we were continually having. However, the main reason was to come up with an ordinance granting the Western Cable TV Company a franchise from the city to install the cable for the television company that Mayor Burns was establishing. After a considerable amount of discussion City Attorney Vehar was directed to look into the situation and work on an ordinance allowing the cable company the right to use streets and public areas for laying cable.

The ordinance was drawn up and introduced by one of the council members. After introduction and advertising, it was the following year before it was passed on final reading. The ordinance drew a lot of interest throughout the community, causing it to be delayed for a few months. The franchise ordinance had to be published in full in the Herald before any more action could be taken on it. At about this same time a new sign ordinance was also being published and acted upon. The sign ordinance was another lengthy ordinance that took a lot of space up in the paper.

Colonel Shiflet had decided that he was coming to Evanston to enter into a lease with the Greater Evanston Development Company. The 10-year lease was initiated and signed by all. Then he said he wanted to immediately apply for the S.B.A. 502 loan through the G.E.D.C. So we got a hold of Larry Goodenough, the S.B.A. representative from Casper, whom we had been working with. Mr. Goodenough said he would come to Evanston and meet with Shiflet to get the application going. They met and completed the application, and Goodenough said he would take it back to Casper and start processing it immediately. Shiflet's request was for one million dollars ($1,000,000). He felt that it would take that much to do the job right. Mr. Goodenough left with the application and Shiflet and the board thanked him and told him that time was essential, that Evanston needed to get the plant opened and in operation.

However, several weeks later Shiflet informed me and the board that he had been denied the S.B.A. financing. When I heard this, it really angered me, so I told the board and Shiflet that I was going to make a trip to Casper right away and find out why his application was denied. I told them that I would go at my own expense.

I immediately called Goodenough to make an appointment with him and possibly one or two of his superiors. Larry Goodenough was a great guy and I know within myself that he probably did all he could to get the application accepted, but I wanted a chance to try to change their mind. If that wasn't possible, I wanted to know exactly why it was denied. Goodenough had no problem with me coming and he set up a meeting between me, him and one of his officers.

When we first met with Shiflet he led us to believe that he had an engineer's degree from the University of Texas and he was a graduate of West Point. He also told us he had other experiences in different engineering projects. He told us that his brother and he had engineered and built a new sewer plant in a town in West Texas. When talking to him he sounded as though he knew all about engineering. The one thing he did tell us that was true, was that he was a retired colonel of the U.S. Army.

When I met with Goodenough and his people in Casper, they told me that when Shiflet filled out his application he had claimed to be a graduate of the University of Texas with an engineer's degree and that he had gone to West Point, but the Small Business Administration could not find any records of that. Then they told me that Shiflet and his brother did engineer a sewer plant, but the plant was not workable and they were being sued by the town that they built the plant for. Well, by the time I got out of that meeting I didn't know what to think, but when I got back to Evanston I informed Mayor Burns and the board of my findings. I don't know exactly how the rest of them felt, but I was pretty depressed by it all, and wasn't looking forward in telling the colonel what I had found.

When I met with Shiflet and told him that there was no way he would ever qualify for a loan with the S.B.A. I told him exactly what they told me. At first I don't think he knew what to say, but he did finally say that he had been to the university and also West Point, but didn't finish. I listened but I didn't really care what he told me at that point, until he finally admitted that he learned engineering while in the army and that he had been in the U.S. Army Corps of Engineers most of his time while in the military. He also said that he and his partner still wanted to open the plant up and get it started. He said his partner had a little money and between them they had enough collateral to get a much smaller loan at the First National Bank, and it would be enough to get the place started.

When I informed the mayor and the board about my meeting with the colonel, they said since we all signed the lease, we might as well let him get started. So when I told Shiflet that we would still go along with him, he said he planned to start hiring employees and get the plant opened up sometime in January. By this time I was feeling a little better about it.

The 10-year lease that was initiated by the G.E.D.C. and the Wyoming Railway Car Company was for only 24 of the 26 acres deeded to the city by the U.P.R.R. The one acre leased to Time-DC and the Palmer house that was sold to the family were deleted from the lease agreement.

Colonel Shiflet was in his late fifties and was very likeable, but you couldn't always believe what he told you. I don't recall his partner's name, but he was an older man, I would guess maybe as much as ten years Shiflet's senior. His partner never took any part in running the plant, but visited quite often.

At the regular meeting in October, the cable TV ordinance was passed on the first reading, and at our regular meeting in November the ordinance was passed on the second reading, all voting in favor. I don't know why, but it wouldn't be until the regular meeting of May, 1974 before the ordinance would be passed on the third reading. I don't recall why there was a delay unless there were a lot of legal problems that needed to be looked into.

At this time, Bridger Valley experienced a small boom caused by the increase of the trona mines west of Green River. A lot of new-comers were living in the valley rather than in Sweetwater County, because it was almost as close as it was to live in Green River or Rock Springs. It was also starting to affect Evanston a little, because some mine employees were also living in Evanston. They would have to commute to the mines, which was a distance of 60 to 75 miles, depending on which mine they worked at. At this time, Evanston's population started growing again and the economy was looking better. In November of that year, the community of Mountain View voted in favor of incorporating and becoming a town. So they made application to incorporate and become their own little community, growing fast because of the trona boom. They were no longer a sub-division of the county. Both Lyman and Mountain View tripled in population in just a few years.

It was then that President Richard Nixon announced that there was an energy shortage, an energy crisis, he called it. He requested that all cities and towns cut down on their Christmas lights. He suggested that they all should be reduced at least 33%. Apparently the entire nation was having an energy shortage. I'm not sure why, but it seemed kind of ridiculous to a lot of people and some thought it might just be another political move. Who knows?

This was about the same time that inflation started getting ridiculously high. Gasoline, coffee, concrete and most all other commodities had taken a big increase in prices. I believe that the 1970s was probably one of the worst periods in American history for inflation. It wasn't long before everything was priced at least ten times the amount it had been in the 1960s. I was under the impression that it was because of the shortage in the energy industry, but again, who knows?

Because of the cable TV ordinance and the sign ordinance, the regular meeting held on November 2nd had to be moved to the Uinta County Courthouse, because so many people were concerned about both ordinances and showed up at the meeting. But once again, the little town hall just wouldn't hold them. We needed a larger city hall and eventually, a few years later, in 1978, we did get one. After hours of discussion on both ordinances the mayor and city council moved back to the city hall council room and acted upon both ordinances, with some amendments, passing on final readings, all voting in favor.

A special meeting was called by the mayor on November 16th to discuss a new subdivision. It was the Kindler Subdivision, presented by Cloey Wall. The ordinance was introduced by one of the council members and the mayor opened the floor up for discussion. After a short discussion it was moved and seconded to be passed on the first reading, all voting in favor. Another special meeting was called by the mayor on November 27th to discuss the police problems we were having and to look at applications for the position of Chief of Police. At this time we had only one application. The council went into executive session to discuss their findings and would announce after the holidays what they had decided.

At our regular meeting on December 4th Mayor Burns was absent, so the president of the council, Mel Baldwin, conducted the meeting. Because of the mayor's absence, other than the normal business, the only other business that came up was the ordinance concerning the Kindler Subdivision. After a lengthy discussion, the city council moved to table the ordinance until a later date. It was suggested that on December 17th we have a joint meeting with the Planning and Zoning Commission for the purpose of discussing the Kindler Subdivision. A motion was made and seconded to have the meeting, all voting in favor.

I don't know why we were having so much trouble with the Kindler Subdivision, unless it was because it was the first major subdivision to come before the city council since the new subdivision ordinance was made into law. I believe every member on the council, including the mayor, and every member of the P & Z Board wanted to be sure everything was in order. The joint meeting was held on December 17th with a lot of discussion, but no other action on the Kindler Subdivision would be taken until the first regular meeting in January, 1974. We also discussed the possibility of having the P & Z Board start working on a comprehensive plan or master plan and have it ready for discussion with the city council by February, 1974.

CHAPTER 8

1974....The first regular council meeting in 1974 was held on January 3rd. More discussion on the Kindler Subdivision was held, but it was the decision of the council to keep it on the table until the regular meeting in February. There were more questions and concerns that the Planning and Zoning Commission had. During the meeting, the council approved the request from P & Z to have the city hire a secretary for their board. The city agreed to pay $25.00 per month for the position. P & Z was meeting once a month at that time.

In January of 1974, Colonel Oliver Shiflet officially opened up the Wyoming Railway Car Company with a ten year renewable lease agreement with the Greater Evanston Development Company, and started out hiring approximately 30 employees. Most of those employees had worked at the U.P. plant prior to it shutting down and were well experienced. Dave Weise, former superintendent of the plant, was hired by Shiflet as a consultant. The headlines of the January 31st issue of the Uinta County Herald read WYO. RAILWAY CAR CO. BEGAN OPERATIONS.

Opening up the plant at this time was a good economic move for Evanston. The city was still in a depressed mode because of the railroad engine crews moving out, but seemed to be gaining population. Anything we could get to come to Evanston that would create additional employment would be a great help to our community, and things were starting to look better.

Shortly after the plant opened, the Union Pacific Railroad Company made an announcement that they would donate all of the railroad tracks within the 26 acres to the city as well. They were originally going to pull all the tracks out, but they decided that the new Wyoming Railway Car Company would have a need for them.

The resolution was made previously to allow the Greater Evanston Development Company to lease the premises from the city and in turn they would sub-lease to the Wyoming Railway Car Company for a period of 10 years with the option to extend. When that resolution was passed, the city also titled all of the loose equipment that the U.P. gave to the city to the G.E.D.C. This was to allow the development company to raise enough money to assist other industries and businesses to apply for the Small Business Administration 502 loan. That loose equipment was sold to the Wyoming Railway Car Company for $7,000.00. The development company used this money to help other businesses and companies that wanted to use the S.B.A 502 program.

As time went on, there were a few that did use it, such as the bowling alley, a body/fender company, a convenience store and fuel station, and several others. All of these new companies provided jobs, which was the whole idea behind the development company: to improve the economy by creating jobs.

Mayor Burns, who was also president of the Wyoming Association of Municipalities, made a report on his trip to San Juan, Puerto Rico where the National League of Cities held their annual convention. He talked a lot about some of the problems cities and towns were having throughout the nation, especially the larger cities, and how federal funding was going to affect various communities.

The Eagle Rock Ski Area finally opened up again that February for the first time since the fire, with everything running well. The turnout was tremendous and everybody seemed to be happy that it was finally opened and the chairlift was working once again.

During our regular meeting in February, the council passed the ordinance concerning the Kindler Subdivision on the 2nd reading with very little discussion. The 3rd and final reading would come up during next month's meeting. Also during this meeting, Cloey Wall, a local surveyor, was named Acting City Engineer since Bert Phillips had left Evanston.

During this time, President Nixon reported that the federal government was still concerned about the energy crisis that the country had experienced during the past few months. He said that because of reports of shortage of fuel for vehicles, the interstate highways in all states would have to reduce the speed limit, which at the time was 70 mph, to 55 mph. The Uinta County Herald newspaper dated February 28th headlines read FEDERAL PRESSURE FORCES WYOMING SPEED LIMITS DOWN TO 55 MPH. There was a lot of controversy throughout the country concerning it, but I guess it did slow the country down and saved on fuel to a certain extent. I don't remember how long the speed limit stayed at 55, but it was a few years. When they did finally raise it, it jumped up to 75 mph.

1974 was the 88th anniversary of the Evanston Voluntary Fire Department. The department held their annual Fireman's Ball that year, plus they had their annual fundraising drive. The volunteer firemen over the years did a tremendous job for Evanston and the surrounding area. They deserved a lot of credit and during that year were highly honored.

At our regular meeting in March, some of the business brought up was that we finally passed the Kindler Subdivision ordinance on the 3rd and final reading with all voting in favor. We also discussed the idea of contracting out the maintenance to the cemetery, but decided against it and kept Tat Titmus on as the sexton. We all felt that it would be better, especially now that we had perpetual care thanks to former Councilman Royce Bills.

The ordinance to allow cable TV was finally passed on the third and final reading during our regular meeting on May 2, 1974 with a motion made by me and seconded by Lunsford. With no other discussion the vote was called, with all voting in favor. This ordinance gave Bob Burns, owner of the new company, Western TV, the right to use the streets and alleys for the purpose of laying and burying TV cable.

During the May meeting Sherman Rollins, who had been acting as Chief of Police for the past several months, presented the mayor with his letter of resignation. He wasn't intending to quit the force, but just wanted to be relieved of the position of Chief. His intentions were to stay on the force as one of the patrolmen. He hoped to be relieved by June 1, 1974. His letter was accepted and the mayor thanked him for his service and assured him he would remain on the force as one of our police officers.

With Rollins resigning right away, it kind of put a rush on hiring someone. Mayor Burns, after reviewing the applications, gave his recommendation. He suggested that the city hire W. David Schrader who for the past four months had served as Administrative Assistant to the Lincoln County Sheriff's Department in Kemmerer, Wyoming. He was 34 years old and was a graduate in law enforcement from the University of California at San Jose. He served for 13 years on the San Jose police department as a patrolman and as Chief of the Investigating Department. He was married and had four children. His résumé was very impressive. After Mayor Burns officially made the appointment, the council all voted in favor to confirm the appointment. Therefore, as he was willing to start immediately, an agreement had been drawn up between him and the city by the attorney for him to start on June 1, 1974. David Schrader was now Chief of Police of Evanston.

From the time that Charles (Chuck) Overy resigned as Chief of Police, Mayor Burns and the council not only appointed Rollins as Acting Chief, he had also appointed officers Edison Lee and Dean Forman as Acting Chief at separate times, for very short periods, after Rollins had resigned. For various reasons, none of them wanted the job, but they were all good officers and stayed with the department.

1974 was another election year for the Mayor and three members of the city council. I was one of those councilmen that were up for re-election. The others were Councilmen Lowell Dawson and Ronald Davis.

Since the time that Colonel Shiflet opened up the Wyoming Railway Car Company, he had been after me to hire me as his General Manager. He must have asked me a dozen times and didn't seem to give up on the idea, so I asked him why he wanted me so badly when he had David Weise, the former U.P. plant superintendent, as a consultant. I said he knows most of the employees. But Shiflet said that he wanted me because I had worked with some of the employees who had been former truck stop workers and that I had the experience of working directly with them, and then he said, *they all seemed to like you and trust you.* Then he told me that he was having problems with the employees, and that the ones that had previously worked at the shops were not all that fond of Weise, because they didn't think that he had made any effort whatsoever in trying to get the railroad to keep the plant open. They felt that he had let all the employees down.

I finally told him that I would talk to my wife Sandy and my brother, and then I would let him know. Sandy left it completely up to me and Bob, my brother and partner, told me to do what I felt was best and said he would be willing to buy me out if I chose to go work at the plant for Shiflet.

In July of that year I met with Shiflet and went over the offer. He told me he would start me out at a salary of $1,200.00 per month (which wasn't bad pay for the times and I had no problem with it), plus a two-week vacation, and that I would have an opportunity to buy into the company anytime I chose to. I told him I was very interested. I said, *on the condition that you are honest and up front with me in all matters pertaining to the business, with no backstabbing or behind-the-back sneaky deals going on with your partner or anyone else. I want everything to be up front between you and me.* I continued, *I assure you that I will be honest with you.* He completely agreed to what I told him and he promised to be fair and honest with me.

After more consideration, I finally made my decision to sell out and take Shiflet up on the deal that he offered me, which I felt was very fair. I was actually looking forward to the change. I was honored that he would think that much of me to offer me the job. I was also looking forward to working with the employees. I knew most of them and knew they were all pretty good workers.

I officially went to work for the colonel in the first part of July. I was to be the general manager of the entire plant and I would be working directly under Shiflet, president of the company. I would be overseeing the employees and helping him sell our services to different railroad companies.

When I got going at the plant and was acquainted with the employees I found out that there were a number of employees who were not very happy with the way things were going. It took me a few weeks to get the employees feeling better about the situation, but there were a couple of welders, good welders, that I had to fire after I found out that they left their job for a few days, without approval, looking for work elsewhere. They ended up working at the trona mines. I don't know why, because the wages being paid at the plant appeared to me to be fair for the type of work being performed, and you didn't have to commute 70 miles to work. Also, the working conditions were good at the plant and most of the workers seemed to be glad they had a job. Most of them were welders and sheet metal workers.

In June, the city started working on the new budget for the fiscal year of 1974 and 1975. Although the economy was getting better and more people were finding jobs, our revenue had not caught up with inflation yet. This meant that we would not be able to approve the budget as presented and would need to cut a good share of the funding that was requested by the departments. We had to concentrate only on the projects that were absolutely necessary. The shortfall on funding was so bad that we had to put a moratorium on the city crews doing any work on sewer and water trenches and mains unless the problem was an emergency. But the good news was that the County Assessor's office showed the assessed value for Uinta County would be way up in the coming year—but it wouldn't be any help until the next fiscal year.

Although revenues were down, Chief Schrader requested a pay raise for the police department. There was no doubt that if we were going to keep any officers at this time we would need to give them some kind of increase in pay, but the mayor said we would put it in the budget and take a good look at it. The budget for 1974-75 was just under $550,000, and was approved by the mayor and council. We were able to give the police department a partial increase, but not what they asked for.

Another problem we were having at this time was a shortage of housing. The Evanston Chamber of Commerce met with city officials.

Evanston now had a lack of living units: rentals and other housing. Since the Wyoming Railway Car Company opened up and the trona mines in Sweetwater County were going strong, other people were starting to move back to Evanston, with no place to live. New subdivisions were being developed, but some of the people were not in a position to qualify for new housing. To qualify for a home at that time, you had to have a sizeable down payment and very good credit. There was no doubt that the housing situation was a big problem.

We were glad the economy was coming back, but until the funding caught up with inflation, it put towns, cities and counties in a very uncomfortable positon when it came to balancing the budget, and by law we had to do that. We could not just assume that the funding would be there.

The 1970s, during Presidents Nixon, Ford and Carter's terms, were very troubling times. This was mostly caused by the Vietnam War going on for such a long time, and the way a lot of the folks were treating the veterans of the Vietnam War when they came home. Some people, including a number of the members of Congress in Washington D.C., forgot how to respect those veterans. They were shameful times for America, patriotism was lacking in many ways, and people were beginning to get the attitude that they just didn't care anymore.

President Nixon promised, when running for election, that he would end the war immediately if elected. Well it took him one full term and part of his second term to end it. The country was going wild and crazy, losing all respect for everything and everybody. The hippy movement was causing problems. Riots and killings throughout the nation were going on. Police were being called "pigs" and other names that were uncalled for. They were losing a lot of respect throughout the country, but they kept trying to do their job the best they could.

To make it even worse, it was a time of serious inflation. All commodities and merchandise were rising in price, some eight to ten times what they were before. Wages and salaries were lagging way behind. Revenues for towns, cities and county governments were also being affected because of a lack of revenue. When prices increased like they did during the 1970s, it hurt everyone because of the time it took income to catch up to the increased prices, especially when prices rose as fast as they did.

Evanston, Wyoming was no different; things were bad here also. Our biggest and best celebration, Cowboy Days, was even getting out of hand. It was getting so bad that a decent person couldn't walk downtown without bumping into a drunk or someone spilling a drink on you, or getting sworn at with the big four-letter "F" word. Our police officers, the few we had, got called all kinds of names, like "pig" or worse, when they would drive by. Camper trailers from out of town were coming into town, and the owners were parking them on downtown streets and bringing prostitution in with them. It was getting so bad that the mayor and city council were getting very concerned, but it was an election year, so there wasn't much done about it just then. It was a bad situation.

Although things weren't going so well, we were still able to hire a few more police officers after Chief Schrader came on board. We knew that Rollins would be retiring soon, so we hired a few more officers during the year. Some of them were Dennis Harvey, Mel Wren, Russell Dean and Forrest Bright.

This being an election year, the mayor and three of the council members had to think about what to expect in the coming years. Those that were running for re-election had to file again during the first part of July, as anyone else that was running had to do. The filing period for running for election expired somewhere around the 6th or 8th of July.

After the filing date expired it was announced that those running for mayor would be incumbent Mayor Robert "Bob" Burns, Dan L. South and Louise H. Karn; for council in Ward 1 would be me and Thomas Gary Bradshaw; Ward 2 would be Lowell R. Dawson unopposed; and Ward 3 would be Ronald O. Davis, Donald D. Rutner and Gary L. Hainley. The primary election was set for August 20, 1974.

I was going to run for the position of mayor this year, but when Burns decided to run for re-election I changed my mind, because in all respect I didn't want to run against the incumbent. I didn't think he was going to run again because of his new cable TV company. I didn't think he would have the time, but rather than run against him I decided to run for re-election to the council. Dawson was also running for re-election to the council. Being unopposed, he would win in the primary and make it into the general election unopposed, unless someone got in by a write-in. Davis was also running for re-election, but he had some competition.

There was a question about Louise Karn's eligibility, because her house had never been annexed into the city. Karn was the wife of Dr. William Karn who was the Superintendent of the Wyoming State Hospital. Although the hospital was in the city limits at the time, her new home was not. When building the new home for the superintendent they located it on the hill across the road from the hospital, putting it out of the city and possibly making her ineligible for the position. A lawsuit was filed.

Other business the city had going that summer was the council passed a resolution to form a Special Improvement District, which would include paving, curbing and gutters and sidewalks for almost every unpaved, unimproved street in the city. It would still leave a few other areas unimproved. Before any bids or action could begin on this project, revenue bonds would have to be sold. This took some time so it was possible we would not get anything done this season. We would have to wait and see.

Also, Chief Schrader got permission to form a Police Reserve Unit, which would involve voluntary personnel from the citizens of the city. His purpose for this was to get additional help to assist his small police department during times like the Uinta County Fair and Cowboy Days. These were very busy times for the city and he needed all the help he could get.

During our regular meeting in August, we discussed the Improvement District some more and the mayor reported that the sale of the bonds was going well. We also discussed the possibility of putting our employees in the Wyoming Retirement Program, but that would have to wait until we saw how the revenues would come in next year. Chief Schrader brought up the idea of setting up a curfew, but that didn't seem to have much support. He did get the council to approve forming a local police commission.

John Proffit and his family moved back to Evanston and went into partnership with Cloey Wall, who was acting as city engineer. They formed a new company called Uinta Engineering and Surveying. We were glad to see Proffit back in town, because we needed an engineer to assist the city with all the subdivisions and developments that had been starting up.

Primary elections were held with Karn and South in the general election for mayor, with South receiving the most votes and Burns receiving the least. However, Mrs. Karn's eligibility was still pending and was in the hands of the Wyoming Supreme Court. Others running in the general election were Bradshaw and me from Ward 1, Dawson unopposed in Ward 2, and Davis and Rutner in Ward 3.

In October things seemed to be picking up at the airport. At the time I wasn't sure why, but there was a lot of exploration for oil and gas going on about this time. This later proved to be very beneficial to many property owners in the area.

Also, this year Albert Pilch was elected president of the Wyoming Recreation Commission, which was good for Evanston, and Mayor Bob Burns was now on the Wyoming Aeronautics Commission. Both positions would help Evanston a lot in the future. Tat Titmus, who had been sexton of the city's cemetery, had retired and Gene Slagowski from public works was named as sexton, taking the place of Titmus.

In September, some interested citizens met with the city council to discuss a better and more complete recreation program for the community. Diane Sather, who had received a degree in recreation from Arizona State University, suggested that the community needed a recreation program that would be effective year round and would serve all ages of Evanston citizens. She was accompanied by her brother, Rick Sather, who was in full support of her request.

After a considerable amount of discussion, Mayor Burns told them that this would be turned over to me and Fife, Councilmen overseeing the city's recreation. I was in favor of the idea of trying to improve our recreation program. My dream, when I was first appointed to recreation after getting elected as a council member, was to build a recreation hall with a large gym, a swimming pool, a weight room and other facilities to benefit folks of all ages. That did become a reality, but several years later.

It was decided that Evanston would form a recreation commission to work on the comprehensive plan that Miss Sather had presented. Some of those citizens that were appointed to the commission, other than me and Fife, were Randy MacDonald, Rick Sather, Denice Wheeler, Mac Smith, Ryley Dawson, my wife Sandy, Gary Bradshaw, Russell "Bub" Albrecht, Mary Richards, Robert Scott, Jerry Wall and Ray Christensen. It was a big board, but all were very interested in the program and it turned out to be a good move.

I outlined the functions of the group during their first meeting, which included working closely with already-organized committees in the community. They also held their first elections during the meeting by voting Randy Mac Donald in as chairman, Rick Sather as vice-chairman and Denice Wheeler as secretary. They decided that the first action to be taken was a survey of the community with the aid of the high school and others.

Chief Schrader gave his police report on Cowboy Days activities. He reported that there were thirty-eight arrests, with eleven of them being issued by the new reserve group. He stated that every officer on the force put in at least 15 hours daily on duty during the three-day event. He also expressed appreciation for the cooperation of the bar and café owners in closing their establishments during altercations and the cooperation of the local citizens in general, saying that there were only three local persons arrested.

He reported that they covered three parades, two alarms, eight ambulance follow-ups and two accidents involving property damage and minor injuries. They handled eight emergency messages, three reports of lost property, one report of a runaway, and one missing person report. They received eight miscellaneous requests for assistance.

They handled five incidents of driving while under the influence of alcohol, twenty incidents of public intoxication and disorderly conduct, six of fighting and breach of peace, four of minors in possession of alcohol, two in possession of a controlled substance, and one contributing to the delinquency of a minor. They accomplished all this with a very small department. Evanston was still short of police officers and would probably need to hire more before next year, because during this celebration things were getting more and more out of hand each year, especially since the state lowered the drinking age to 19. Chief Schrader said that the lower drinking age was causing a good share of the problem.

From the report it appeared that the police department had a busy three days, and thankfully no one was hurt. Mayor Burns thanked him for such a thorough report and requested that he pass on to the department the council's appreciation for their service during the three-day event.

At a hearing conducted on October 11th in Evanston, the Third District Court Judge C. Stuart Brown ruled that Mrs. Louise Karn *is not eligible to hold municipal office in Evanston because of residency requirements.* The lawsuit was filed by a large group of Evanston citizens against Mrs. Karn and in support of Mayor Bob Burns. The headlines of the Uinta County Herald issue of October 17th read, COURT DECLARES MRS. KARN INELIGIBLE TO SEEK OFFICE OF MAYOR IN EVANSTON.

With the disqualification of Karn, who won in the primaries, incumbent Mayor Burns would now become eligible to run in the election against Dan South and seek re-election during the general election, which would be held on November 5th.

I felt bad for Louise, because I believe she would have been good for Evanston if she would have had a chance to run, but the courts declared her ineligible. I'm sure this was a big disappointment to her and her constituents.

The General Elections were over now and Dan South was elected as Evanston's new mayor. The Uinta County Herald dated November 7th read, DAN SOUTH IS NEW MAYOR OF EVANSTON. I got re-elected as City Councilman, and both Lowell Dawson and Ron Davis were re-elected. South beat Burns by a large margin, which was no surprise because Burns came in last during the primary election. Karn received 124 write-in votes.

I was a little disappointed that Burns didn't make it because I thought he had done a good job as mayor, especially in his first 6 years. During that period he had pioneered ordinances such as planning and zoning, the subdivision and development ordinances, plus a new sign ordinance, and he got the railroad to donate the roundhouse with 26 acres of property to the city. He also had a big part in getting the Wyoming Railway Car Company started. He was mayor during some very troubling times for the city, and through his efforts he made Evanston into a First Class City. Bob just had too many things to think about the last two years, such as getting his new cable TV company going, being appointed to the Wyoming Aeronautics Commission, and being president of the Wyoming Association of Municipalities during the 1973-74 year.

However, I believe the biggest thing that hurt him was the cable TV company. If anyone else had brought cable to Evanston, they probably would have been very well accepted, but because he was mayor some people thought that he used his position to get the franchise. I don't believe him being mayor had anything to do with it. He was simply in the right position to be able to get the business going.

Dan South took office as Evanston's mayor in January of 1975. I looked forward to serving under him and thought that he would do a good job. I had known Dan since high school, and we had been pretty close friends over the years. Anyway, I congratulated him and told him if he needed anything from me not to hesitate to ask.

Also, that year Ed Herschler was elected as Governor of Wyoming, beating Dick Jones in the general election. Herschler was an attorney from Kemmerer and was well known throughout Western Wyoming. He replaced Governor Hathaway, who did not seek re-election that year.

CHAPTER 9

1975....The regular meeting held in January 1975 was opened by Melvin Baldwin, president of the council, because Mayor Burns, for reasons unknown, did not show up. The first order of business was the swearing in of the new mayor and councilmen. J. P. Hudson, City Clerk, performed the swearing-in ceremony. After Dan South was sworn in as mayor, Baldwin presented the gavel to him and he proceeded to conduct the meeting.

South gave a short speech showing his appreciation for being elected, then spoke on some of his ideas on how he wanted to improve the community, and then he proceeded with the regular business. His first order of business was, of course, the approval of the minutes from the previous meeting and the approval of the bills that were to be paid.

Following the regular business, Mayor South made the following appointments: J. P. (Percy) Hudson, City Clerk and Treasurer; David Schrader, Chief of Police; and John Proffit, City Engineer. After the election, with Burns going out, Vincent Vehar resigned as city attorney.

Mayor South continued by appointing the council members to their respective departments with basically the same assignments as the previous year. Fife and I were still overseeing Recreation and also the water department. A new Recreation and Education Commission had been formed and they were starting to work on the proposed master plan that was presented to them by Diane Sather. They planned to meet on January 22nd to elect their officers, but mainly to approve their proposed Operations Manual, Constitution and By-laws. Randy Mac Donald, president of the commission, stated that the manual and other documents would be presented to the Evanston City Council for their approval at their next regular meeting on February 4th.

Bernard Gram, Civil Defense Director for the county, presented the city with a large snow plow from the inventories of Civil Defense equipment salvaged from World War II leftover supplies. We weren't sure whether it had been used or not, but it was very much needed and looked like it would do the job. Mayor South showed his appreciation, and so did the street crew, Buff Bruce, Allen Kennedy and Jack Day, because the city equipment was getting worn out and the city didn't have a lot of money at that time.

The economy was starting to look better, revenues were slowly increasing, but population was growing faster than expected, and the town limits were expanding. This caused Evanston's need for additional and upgraded street equipment, more water and sewer lines, additional police officers and patrol cars and other equipment, and additional employees. We still had the problems because revenues were not coming in fast enough to take care of the growth and our immediate needs. The community was just changing too fast.

Mayor South called for a special meeting on January 13, 1975 for the purpose of meeting with the County Attorney and the Police Department to discuss the article published by the Police Chief in the December 19, 1974 issue of the Uinta County Herald, titled INDIVIDUALS WILL NOT BE PROSECUTED.

Apparently, County Attorney Charles Phillips was bothered by the article because it indicated that no individual would be prosecuted through his office regardless of the evidence, while the article was actually talking about one individual case where such prosecution was not economically feasible and was thrown out because of a lack of evidence. The case was discussed by the County Attorney, the Sheriff and members of the Evanston Police Department who, after examining the evidence, all agreed that the case should be dismissed.

Chief Schrader felt pretty bad about the entire situation and explained to those present that he had no control over the wording of the article published in the paper. He gave the information to the reporter and she apparently worded the story to suit herself. He also said that it was not his intention to cast any reflections or say anything derogatory about Mr. Phillips and that he would publicly apologize for the article, and he did. Mr. Phillips thanked the council for their time and stated that it was not his intention to criticize the police, but to criticize the published article. Mayor South thanked him and said he hoped nothing like this would ever happen again.

At this time we were without a city attorney but Mayor South approached Ted Ellingford, another local attorney, to accept the position as Evanston's city attorney. The mayor asked him to be present at this meeting and state his feelings about accepting the position. Mr. Ellingford was in attendance and told the council that he wanted the council to first know that he also was representing the Town of Lyman at the present. However, he said he would accept the position as Evanston's city attorney either on a retainer's fee or at an hourly basis. After some questions and concerns from the council, I made the motion, seconded by Lunsford, that Ellingford be employed on a retainer fee of $400.00 per month, January through June of that year (1975). Motion passed with all voting in favor. We now had an attorney to represent the city.

Chief Schrader presented a paper outlining things that the department had accomplished and things he hoped to accomplish. The council largely agreed to his proposals and thanked him for his efforts. However, some of the council had problems with the way the police department was publishing their police report in the paper each week, so a motion was made and seconded to direct the city clerk to furnish the newspaper with only the monthly police justice report, all voting in favor.

Chief Schrader also requested the council's permission to return items that had been stolen from the recent break-in of the police office. The police office at that time was one small room in the Old Town Hall building with very little security. Items taken were one hundred dollars in cash that had been stolen from the A. A. Texaco Station in a recent burglary, now being held by the police for evidence, and a shotgun belonging to the police department. A motion was made by Councilman Dawson, seconded by me. The motion passed with five yes votes and one abstention. One councilman, who was on the police commission, abstained from voting, because he felt that he had a conflict.

At our regular meeting of February 4th some of the same old problems came up, such as downtown parking and meters not operating properly. The city was in the process of leasing the old Y.M.C.A. property owned by the railroad on the corner of 11th and Front Street (Martin Park is located there at the present). The Y.M.C.A. building had been torn down, leaving the property vacant. The railroad agreed to lease the property to the city so the city could then turn it into a public parking lot. This would help with some of the parking, but a lot of the parking meters were not working properly so we had to replace some of them. The two-hour parking ordinance was still in effect and being enforced.

There was a mention of traffic lights, but the only traffic light at that time was the one on the intersection of 11th and Summit Streets. That was there mainly because of the schools that were in that vicinity. There was a request for a traffic light on the intersection of 9th and Front Street, but that didn't come until later. The parking and traffic problem was getting worse, but studies were being done by the Wyoming Highway Department consistently, and Councilman Baldwin informed the group that a master plan for Evanston was in the making by the Planning and Zoning Commission.

The folks that lived in the downtown area, where parking meters were installed, were allowed to use a meter hood furnished by the city to be able to have free parking when necessary. Sometimes this was difficult because the meters in front of their residence may have already been taken, so it didn't work out well all the time. Downtown parking was getting to be more of a problem all the time, but studies and plans were being looked into constantly.

Petitions for annexation were getting to be a quite a problem. Subdivisions outside the present city limits were being planned and presented to the council for approval. The community was not only growing in population but was also growing in area, creating new streets, new water and sewer lines that the city had to maintain. This was a problem because our revenues were not meeting the additional needs. In some cases, the cost of laying the water and sewer lines had to be paid by the city, causing a real budget problem. At this time we had to do a lot of transferring of funds in the already short budget.

Our sewer plant was getting so bad that we had to hire an additional employee, Fay Riebennacht, to be at the plant most of the time. He was already living in a mobile home and requested permission to move the home to the property of the sewer plant so he could keep a better watch on the plant in case any of the equipment started acting up. It was the consensus of the council to allow him to do this provided he paid the water and sewer rates like everyone else, plus if he ever quit or transferred to another department he would have to immediately move his home. That spring, during one of the meetings, Mayor South made new assignments for the members of the council. He declared a three-man police commission, naming himself as Commissioner and council members Fife and Dawson on the commission. The street commissioner would be Jon Lunsford, assisted by Ron Davis; water commissioner would be Dawson, assisted by me; commissioner over cemetery would be Davis, assisted by Baldwin. Planning and Zoning was assigned to Baldwin, assisted by Dawson; sanitation commissioner would be Mayor South, assisted by Fife. Airport was given to Davis, who would also be a member of the Airport Board. Recreation was assigned to me again, and the fire department was assigned to Lunsford, mainly because he was a member of the department.

Mayor South also expressed his opinion on the annual Cowboy Days celebration. He stated that it seemed to be getting out of control and needed to be cleaned up. The means of doing this were to be decided upon in the coming months before the next celebration. He also called for a meeting of all city employees to discuss with them the problems and needs confronting the city.

At this time Evanston and Uinta County weren't the only ones having growing and financial problems, mostly because of the increased production of the trona mines in Sweetwater County. Kemmerer and Lincoln County were also having the same problems, so a Lincoln and Uinta County planner, Mr. Glen Payne, was hired to assist both counties. Through this association between counties Payne was to help by working on a comprehensive study of water quality planning and water pollution control, and applying for a grant from the Federal Water Pollution Control Act if needed. Both counties and all communities helped in funding the program.

At the May 6th city council meeting Councilman Dawson introduced a resolution titled: RESOLUTION CONCERNING COOPERATION WITH THE LINCOLN, UINTA COUNTIES PLANNING OFFICE, which required the Lincoln and Uinta County offices to provide planning support to the City of Evanston as well as the rest of the county. The resolution was passed with all voting in favor.

At this same meeting Chief Schrader informed the council that Officer Sherman Rollins was retiring after 21 years of service to the city. He stated that a retirement dinner was being planned at The Last Outpost Café on May 17th and that the mayor and all council members were invited to attend. He also asked the council to participate in funds to buy Rollins a nice retirement gift. All voted in favor of helping out.

During the May 6th meeting more ordinances were voted on and passed. Ordinance #306, concerning the "Gas Installation Code"; Ordinance #300, creating the "Evanston Recreation Board" and accepting their constitution and by-laws; Ordinance #301, "Establishing the Manner of Driving Vehicles"; and Ordinance #302, defining "Loitering and Minor," "Curfew Hours," and "Public Place." Also passed was Ordinance #303, "Prohibiting the Sale of Alcoholic or Malt Beverages to any Habitual Drunkard, Incompetent Person or Person under the Age of 19 Years," and Ordinance #307, "Annexing a Certain Territory Known as 'Valley View Addition' to the City of Evanston." It was a busy night, but a lot got accomplished.

At this time I was still working as General Manager at the Wyoming Railway Car plant and getting along well with Colonel Shiflet. We had plenty of railway cars to repair and renovate, mostly hopper types from the trona mines in Sweetwater County. Things were looking good, and Shiflet tried a couple more times for the S.B.A. 502 loan, but never could qualify, so he went ahead and started the business as you might say, "on a shoestring." He was doing a great job repairing the cars and his customers seemed to be well satisfied because they kept sending cars to the plant for repairs. He may not have had a college degree in engineering, but by damn, he appeared to know what he was doing.

F.M.C. from over at the West Vaco mine was having problems with a bunch of aluminum hopper cars. They were about to junk them and get other cars to replace them because they started swaying at the bottom. They had a couple dozen or more of them when Shiflet got talking to the top manager at F.M.C., I don't recall his name, about the cars. Shiflet told them to hold off and he would come up with a blueprint on how he could repair the cars for far cheaper than the cost of new ones, plus they would last for years. They agreed to give him the time.

When the Colonel got back to the plant he told me about it and took me and showed what he was going to propose. He drew up a blueprint of how he could take those aluminum cars and have them cambered and make them much stronger. His plan was to split those cars down the middle from one side at the bottom to the other side at the bottom. Then he would take a sheet of aluminum and cut a piece in the shape of a large wedge and weld it to each side of the car, cambering the floor and causing an upward curve to it. The piece of aluminum would be cut at the top about nine inches and the bottom would come to a point. After that was complete he would weld a piece of aluminum at the open gap on top. He said this would make the car much more usable and stronger than ever.

He took this plan and talked to the management at the F.M.C. plant and sold them on the idea. They were very excited about it and gave him the contract to go ahead. He told them that he had plenty of welders that were well qualified to weld aluminum. It worked out well and we got all their aluminum cars to camber the floor. The Colonel always seemed to know what he was talking about.

Shiflet wanted to expand his work and go visit other car companies and railroads to get to work on their cars. He had gone to a few places by himself and was very successful, but later on he took me with him to get what he called some experience. He took me to Chicago with him to talk to the Northern Tank Car Company, and for the first time we were able to get tank cars to work on—and plenty of them. Actually, they were very dangerous to weld on because of the type of material they hauled, but we always made sure they were cleaned out.

And then he took me with him to Vancouver, Canada and met with a couple of Canadian companies. One was Lithcote Corporation. We had a little trouble getting some of the railroad company's cars, mainly because they were all union, and the Wyoming Railway Car Company was not a union shop. This caused some problems, but for some reason or other we were able to overcome that, because we did get a few cars from Canada.

Late that year he sent me by myself to a small town north of Sacramento, California where Western Pacific was located. While there, I talked to the top people and told them about our program. They seemed to be very interested, but the union situation came up again. They still talked as though they would be willing to send some of their cars to us. I left feeling pretty good, but a little worried. However, it wasn't very long after I got back to the plant, after filling the Colonel in on my visit with them and what they said, that we got a call from them saying that they would be glad to send some of their cars to us.

I really enjoyed working for the Colonel. He taught me a lot about the business, but I never did learn how to weld; I don't know why unless it was because I was more involved with the management, and that was taking plenty of my time. However, the railway plant has been a good industry for Evanston with good, high paying jobs at a time when the city needed a boost in the economy.

This was also the time of year that the mayor and council had to start working on the budget for the fiscal year of 1975-76 which had to be advertised, a date set for a public hearing and then acted on and passed prior to July 1st. All departments had been instructed to get their budget requests in to the city treasurer early. As usual, we had to do a lot of cutting in all departments because, once again, the anticipated revenues were not going to come in high enough to meet all that was requested by the department heads. After a lot of discussion and concern by the departments and the public, the fiscal year budget was passed at a total of $789,334, the highest budget to date the city had ever called for. The county assessor's office indicated to us that we would probably have another increase in revenue for the next year if the county kept growing. Evanston was now close to 5,000 in population.

On June 24th at 7:30 p.m., a swearing-in ceremony was held for members of the newly formed Evanston Police Reserve Unit. The oath was administered by Mayor Dan South to eight members: Mac Smith, Craig Nelson, Jack Wilson, Sonny Blakeslee, Larry Hendrix, Scott Thompson, my son Rand Ottley and Joe Fessenden, as reserve commander. As a member of the city council and a member of the Wyoming Planning on Criminal Administration I was also in attendance. Others attending the ceremony were Jake Williams as reserve coordinator agent, Chief Dave Schrader, and Officers Dean Forman and Mel Wren. Reserve officers Dick Whittaker, Kevin Smith, Jon Lunsford and Norm Newlon were sworn in at a later date.

These officers were a volunteer force that received continuous training covering search and seizure procedures, firearms, narcotics, investigative techniques, first aid, techniques of laws and arrest, police procedures, booking and report writing, defense tactics, pursuit driving, Wyoming state statutes and municipal ordinances. Chief Schrader stated that all members of the unit would have to furnish their own equipment and volunteer their training time without pay. He also stated that the unit would be a big asset for the department in trying to control the crowd during the Cowboy Days celebration.

At our regular meeting on July 2nd, more new subdivision plats were presented for council approval, causing hours of discussion, and in addition the following ordinance prepared by the attorney was read in full. The title of Ordinance #310 was, "An Ordinance Restricting Places for Consumption or Possession in Open Containers and Providing a Penalty for Violation"; this is the so-called "Open

Container Ordinance" that the mayor and council had tried to get passed prior to the 1975 Cowboy Days celebration.

However, the council was reluctant to take any action on the ordinance during this meeting because of the late hour, and they felt there were additional changes and additions that should be discussed before presenting it to the public. Being as it hadn't even been introduced yet, it was tabled until we had more time to discuss it. It was getting late in the year, and I, along with other members of the council, didn't think we would get anything done on the ordinance or even get it on the table for discussion before the Labor Day weekend. I think we were all hoping that this year's celebration would be a lot calmer and better controlled with the newly organized Police Reserve Unit being involved.

That August the Evanston Recreation Board started work on a recreation site jointly with the Purple Sage Golf Course and the Ladies Literary Club. The site was adjacent to the golf course and would include a driving range for golfers, an archery range, shuffle board courts, horse shoe pits, a playground and a picnic area. All labor was donated by a large number of local citizens and was used for in-kind matching for funds through the Wyoming Recreation Commission. It was a community project and any and all voluntary help from the public was very much appreciated. Because of the in-kind match, no local tax dollars were used.

J. P. (Percy) Hudson, who had held the position of City Clerk and Treasurer for over nineteen years, made the announcement that he would be retiring on August 1, 1975. He had started with former Mayor Robert Hamblin in 1956 when Evanston was still considered a town. In all his years of service he had the remarkable record of never having missed a single city council meeting, and he had never been late with a monthly report. I had served as councilman for almost nine years during his time with the city. I learned a lot from him and appreciated his association very much.

On the day Percy retired he turned over all his responsibilities to Don U. Welling, who was appointed by Mayor South and confirmed by the council to succeed him in office. After the swearing in of Mr. Welling we now had a new City Clerk and Treasurer. It was a change that we all had to get used to, but we felt that Welling was capable of handling the position and we were looking forward to be working with him.

Mayor South had appointed me to the Evanston Cowboy Days Committee earlier that year, but when I went to the first meeting, the members indicated that they did not take members by appointments anymore, that their members were picked at random by the members of the committee. Galen Myers was chairman and I said to him, *Well, if that's the case, I will just leave and inform the mayor that your committee has changed the way you now receive members.* When I got up to leave, Chairman Myers spoke up and said, *hold on and let's stop and think about this before turning him down. He has been on the committee for several years in the past, and he may be an asset to the program. He may have some good ideas that may help us,* he continued, and I suggest that we accept his appointment, because it's not like we have too many members. With that they elected me to remain on the committee, as if I needed another job.

Labor Day that year landed on September 1st, so our Cowboy Days celebration was held on August 30th, 31st and September 1st, and it turned out to be worse than the previous year. There was never much problem at the fairgrounds where the rodeo took place, but all the problems seemed to take place in downtown Evanston, where the activity was before, during and after the rodeo. The committee had a dance downtown along with other games and fun activities for families to enjoy, but there were also several bars downtown.

Front Street, for two blocks, was packed with people carrying open cans, bottles and glasses of drinks from the bars, some drunker than others, staggering down the street, sometimes spilling drinks on people when bumped into and sometimes calling them foul names using the big "F" word among other uncalled-for names. Most of these people getting abused were downtown just trying to have a good time with their family, playing the games and trying to enjoy other available fun events.

Main Street and 10th Street weren't much different. Folks from out of town brought camper trailers and parked them downtown on

Main Street and 10th Street near the bars. When walking by these parked campers, you could see the units bouncing and rocking. It didn't take an adult long to figure out what was going on inside those units. Yes, it was prostitution, illegal as it was, happening right in downtown Evanston. Our police officers, including the reserve officers, were having a tough time even trying to enforce the law. They were getting called pigs and other rotten names, and some of the drunks were throwing beer cans, bottles and glasses at them.

There were incidents where drunks were urinating right off the curbs where people were trying to enjoy themselves. Decent folks and their families were witnessing this sort of thing. There were also loud drunks staggering around on the streets with their drinks in hand, using language uncalled for among kids and most adults. The bars were jammed so there was a lot of drinking on the streets which was causing a lot of problems. It didn't seem like we had too many people badly hurt, thank God, but there had been several fights that the police were called in to break up. The police were all over, watching the situation the best they could, but they were also trying to stay as inconspicuous as possible to keep from having any more problems than we were already having.

Being on the committee, John Stevens and I were assigned to oversee the dance that was held downtown on Main Street. We roped off about half the block close to 9th Street and wrapped off an area with canvas, leaving an entranceway where folks could buy a ticket and get in to dance and enjoy the music. We had hired a great band that was local and well known. The program started out real good and everyone was enjoying the dance when a bunch of young people, some locals, some half drunk, sneaked in under the canvas. Some started tearing it down trying to get into the dance area. This incident almost caused a riot, but the police and their reserve unit came and got everything calmed down. A few arrests were made.

It was a bad year for the famous Evanston Cowboy Days celebration—probably the worst yet, but prior to the event Chief Schrader told the council that the biggest problems were caused by young people between the ages of 18 and 21 from out of town. He said that those from Utah came up to have a good time because our legal drinking age was 19. He said, *They have a little trouble handling themselves, and their idea of fun is not the same as ours.* Most of us agreed with him, but we told him there were other problems besides just young kids drinking. The biggest problem was that we had let this sort of thing go on too long without trying to do something about it.

Several residents living in the area of Main Street and Front Street had reported their desire to abolish Cowboy Days entirely. Some residents had said that drunks had been carousing around vomiting on their lawns and porches, and had even reported sex acts being performed in the street and in yards. They stated that something had to be done, that things like this cannot go on.

At the September 3rd meeting, just after the celebration, Chief Schrader told the council that this year he even had to call in the highway patrol, some of the Uinta County Sheriff's deputies, and five officers from Lincoln County. Without their assistance and without the Police Reserve to help, things would have been a lot worse, because the problems were not just confined to the downtown area. The problem was all over Evanston.

He stated that two things needed to be done: the open container ordinance needed to be passed and restrictions on camper trailer units needed to be restricted from downtown areas, including campers attached to pickups, because there was no doubt that they were being used for prostitution.

Mayor South expressed his concern for the safety of police officers and other law enforcement officers during the city's annual Cowboy Days celebration, and told the chief to extend the council's appreciation to all those law enforcement officers that assisted in controlling things over the Labor Day weekend celebration.

Uinta County Herald

Volumn 41, Number 47   EVANSTON, WYOMING 82930   THURSDAY, NOVEMBER 20, 1975   Price 15c Per Copy

Open Container Ordinance Will Face Final Reading Nov. 25th

The third and final reading of Evanston's proposed open container ordinance will take place at a special meeting at 7 p.m. November 25th in the council chambers.

Councilman Dennis Ottley says that this meeting is designed to give everyone a chance to speak out before the ordinance is adopted. He urges anyone interested in the ordinance to be in attendance.

He said, "My opinion is that this is a good ordinance. Of course, any ordinance is only as good as its enforcement."

He indicated that similar ordinances have served well in quite a number of major Wyoming cities.

He said, by way of providing background for the proposed ordinance, that Cowboy Days in Evanston has become "quite a problem". The new nineteen year old drinking age has also contributed to increasing the problem, according to Ottley. He indicated that the Front Street area in particular has become a severe problem during the annual Labor Day weekend cele-

that it had to do something. But it is hard to know what the solution is." He says that this ordinance is the best solution that anyone has come up with to solve the crowds of drinkers milling around Front Street during Cowboy Days.

The celebration has come to be one associated with fighting and other illegal activities, according to reports by Evanston residents living in the area. They have said that drinking youth come during that weekend to take advantage of Wyoming's low drinking age. Other people also come to Evanston to "Let off steam," according to reports by Evanston residents.

The ordinance was originally introduced by Dennis Ottley, with the assistance of the city attorney. Ottley says he has checked with several cities in his efforts to set up an effective ordinance.

He said the ordinance was passed on its two readings unanimously.

"If and when it is made law, a sign will be made by the city stating the ordinance and its

number," he said. "The sign will be posted at eye level by anyone holding a liquor license."

He said that, among the many cities having such an organization, are Jackson, Cheyenne, Rock Springs, and Casper. He said that mayor Dan South is fully in favor of the ordinance, as is the attorney general.

He emphasized that liquor sellers will not be held responsible for violations of the ordinance.

The ordinance reads:

ORDINANCE NO. 313

An ordinance prohibiting the sale or dispensing of alcoholic or malt beverages in open containers for off premise consumption and prohibiting the possession or consumption of alcoholic and malt beverages in open containers while operating a motor vehicle and on sidewalks, curbs, streets, and in other public areas designated by the governing body of the City of Evanston, and providing a penalty thereof.

Be it ordained by the governing body of the City of Evanston, Wyoming:

Section 1: It shall be unlawful for any person to sell or dispense alcoholic or malt beverages in open containers from the licensed facilities used to serve customers for off premise consumption; commonly referred to as drive up window.

Section 2: It shall be unlawful for any person to consume alcoholic or malt beverages from an open container while operating a motor vehicle.

Section 3: It shall be unlawful for any person to consume or carry any alcoholic or malt beverages in an open container while upon any public street, sidewalk, curb, or other public areas as designated by the governing body of the City of Evanston.

Section 4: Open container is defined as any glass, cup, bottle, can or other receptacle used for drinking which is not sealed or capped.

Section 5: Any person found guilty of violating this ordi-

Councilman Dennis Ottley introduced open container proposal.

nance shall be deemed guilty of a misdemeanor and shall be fined not more than $200.

Ottley says that even if changes are made at this final reading, the ordinance will not have to go through another series of readings. He indicated that it is therefore important that interested persons attend the meeting even if they have already attended one of the previous meetings.

Our regular city council meeting wasn't held until a few days after the Cowboy Days celebration was over. The meeting held on September 3rd and after Chief Schrader gave his report on the police problems and activities during the celebration, Mayor South said we had to do something about these problems. He said that we had Ordinance #310 concerning the open container situation and we tabled it, letting it die, but the attorney has drawn up another, which will be Ordinance #313. At that time he had the ordinance read by title only with copies furnished to all present.

ORDINANCE 313: AN ORDINANCE PROHIBITING THE SALE OR DISPENSING OF ALCOHOLIC OR MALT BEVERAGES IN OPEN CONTAINERS FOR OFF-PREMISES CONSUMPTION AND PROHIBITING THE POSSESSION OR CONSUMPTION OF ALCOHOLIC AND MALT BEVERAGES IN OPEN CONTAINERS IN MOTOR VEHICLES AND PROVIDING A PENALTY THEREFORE.

After the ordinance was read Mayor South asked the council for someone to introduce it. He said we needed to get this introduced before we could have any discussion or act on it. It didn't appear at first that anyone wanted to take the responsibility of introducing it so after a few moments I spoke up and said; *I'll introduce Ordinance 313 so we can get it on the floor for discussion*. At that time Mayor South opened the ordinance up for discussion.

Mr. J. D. Kindler, one of the local liquor dealers, spoke up and suggested that maybe the Cowboy Days celebration should be abolished. He stated that he didn't think that an ordinance should be passed just for a special time of a celebration. A lengthy discussion followed, and the council was concerned that if we didn't do something to settle those people down that drink and party a lot, locals as well as those from out of town, things would get worse and we would be forced to abolish Cowboy Days. There had been some folks out there that had suggested just that, especially if the celebration continues to be the way it had been the past few years with every year getting worse, especially since they lowered the drinking age to 19.

However, it was said that Cowboy Days had been a great event for Evanston in the past and we would all like it to continue as a fun family celebration. Evanston is well known for its great Cowboy Days event. After discussion, a motion made by Councilman Lunsford with a second by Councilman Dawson to pass Ordinance #313 on first reading, all voting in favor, the motion passed. Mayor South then announced that the second reading would be acted upon during the next regular city council meeting in October.

Before the meeting ended with other business taken care of, Chief Schrader expressed his appreciation for the passing of the open container ordinance on the first reading and hoped it would be finalized on the third reading. He stated that it would help his forces to keep law and order. The chief was then commended by the council for the efficient and orderly manner in which his forces worked during Cowboy Days.

Previously, the mayor and city council had promoted Allen Kennedy as the General Foreman of public works. Kennedy had been with the street department in the past, but things were getting so out of hand and the community was changing so fast that we felt that some adjustments needed to be done. Buff Bruce, at that time, was overseeing streets. Kennedy, with his new position, was required to attend all council meetings with his report.

The next regular council meeting was held on November 4th with all members of the council and city officials present, plus a group of interested citizens. After the mayor called for motions approving the previous minutes and the payment of the bills, he opened the meeting for business.

Glenn Payne, the Lincoln-Uinta County Planner, met with the council to review a meeting held recently with the planning committee about some grant moneys received for the county and city. Other issues that came up concerned variances, trading of property, speeding problems on certain streets, hiring additional employees, problems with the golf course well, and it was reported by Chief Schrader that a bomb threat at the Evanston Junior High School had been made, but nothing happened; it appeared to be a hoax. He also mentioned the report that literature was being sold to school-age children that bordered on pornographic. He assured the council that this would be investigated.

Attorney Harry Lee Harris was present at the meeting representing the Evanston Liquor Dealers. He made a presentation regarding an amendment to Ordinance #313 as the ordinance came up for second reading. His two proposal were presented with a discussion following. J. Wilburn Bowns and A. G. Spencer, who were also in attendance, voiced their opinion and complemented the mayor and council for wanting to pass some kind of legislation that will help control Cowboy Days and possibly other events in the future.

At that time I made a motion that was seconded by Lunsford to amend Ordinance #313 to read as follows:

AN ORDINANCE PROHIBITING THE SALE OR DISPENSING OF ALCOHOLIC OR MALT BEVERAGES IN OPEN CONTAINERS FOR OFF-PREMISE CONSUMPTION AND PROHIBITING THE POSSESSION OR CONSUMPTION OF ALCOHOLIC AND MALT BEVERAGES IN OPEN CONTAINERS WHILE OPERATING A MOTOR VEHICLE, ON SIDEWALKS, CURBS, STREETS AND OTHER PUBLIC AREAS DESIGNATED BY THE GOVERNING BODY OF THE CITY OF EVANSTON, AND PROVIDING A PENALTY THEREFORE, OR IT ORDAINED BY THE GOVERNING BODY OF THE CITY OF EVANSTON, WYOMING.

The motion was passed as amended, unanimously on second reading, all voting in favor.

Before adjourning, Mayor South announced that there will be two special meetings in November. The first would be scheduled for November 14th. This meeting would be to discuss the possible formation of a new Improvement District in the city to construct paved streets, curbing and gutters in areas such as the Crompton Addition off County Road and the Bateman Addition just off Park Road. Residents of the area requested the meeting, but all citizens of interest are invited to attend.

The meeting was held, with the project being presented by John Proffit, City Engineer. After a considerable amount of discussion, it was the decision of all citizens involved in the Improvement District for the city to proceed with the sale of bonds and begin immediately with the improvements of the streets. Council did not take action at this meeting, but it would be acted upon during the regular meeting in December. The meeting was adjourned.

The other special meeting was held on November 25th for the purpose of allowing the public to voice their opinion concerning the proposed open container ordinance, ORDINANCE #313. This ordinance had already been passed on first and second readings. Mayor South stated that the third reading and final vote by the council would be scheduled for this meeting.

At the November 25th meeting a large crowd of interested citizens attended, including Attorney Harry Lee Harris representing the Evanston Liquor Dealers Association. It was quite a long meeting with everyone getting to state their concerns. The mayor assured the crowd that the ordinance was not to be passed to curtail anyone's freedom, but to give the city some leverage to control large events and rowdy crowds that get out of hand.

During discussion a number of citizens were concerned about certain areas in the city that they felt should be exempt from the ordinance, such as the Purple Sage Golf Course, Hamblin Park, and the Uinta County Fair Grounds, while others questioned the validity of some of the sections in the ordinance. But City Attorney Ted Ellingford assured those present that he had made a special effort to be sure of the legality of the entire ordinance and that he felt that it was very valid and was enforceable. Some wondered if the ordinance could be written to refer to only certain events and enforced only on special occasions. Both attorneys, Ellingford and Harris, said that it may be unconstitutional as it bordered on selective enforcement.

During the meeting, Mayor South said that the city would make up notices concerning the ordinance and that the wording would be condensed down for easy reading. He said with the cooperation of the liquor dealers, the notices would be posted in all bars at eye level to inform their patrons of the ordinance, making them aware of the ordinance before carrying an open container drink out of the establishment.

It was getting late and it appeared that everyone had their chance to express their opinion concerning the ordinance, so the mayor ceased all discussion. I felt after listening to all of the discussion and concerns from the public that the majority of those present realized that something had to be done.

After South ended discussion, he called for the council to act on the passage of the ordinance. At that time Councilman Baldwin made a motion to amend the ordinance by adding a paragraph that would make an exception of certain areas. Those areas would be the Uinta County Fairgrounds, the Purple Sage Golf Course and Hamblin Park. The motion was seconded by Councilman Dawson. A roll call vote was called with the following result: Fife, aye; Lunsford, aye; Baldwin, aye; Ottley, aye; Dawson, aye; Councilman Davis was not present, therefore he did not vote. The motion passed with five voting aye.

With the amendment being passed, I made a motion that Ordinance #313 be accepted and passed as amended on the third and final reading, seconded by Lunsford. Again, Mayor South called for a roll call vote. The vote was as follows: Lunsford, aye; Ottley, aye; Baldwin, aye; Dawson, aye; and Fife, nay. Mr. Davis was not present. With four ayes and one nay the majority ruled in favor of passing Ordinance #313 on final reading, making it effective immediately. The mayor then thanked all those present for coming and for expressing their concerns, and thanked the council for their actions and then adjourned the meeting.

The following issue of the Uinta County Herald article read, OPEN CONTAINER LAW ADOPTED. It was now law, but some people were concerned with how it was going to be enforced. This was a problem for the police department and the mayor and city council members. They were also concerned, but over the years it seemed to quiet things down a bit, though some of the liquor dealers were still upset. And to this day some people are still blaming me because I introduced the ordinance.

However, that didn't bother me then and it doesn't bother me now, because, at the time, it was something that was badly needed.

Under the same circumstances I would have done the same thing. Since then, over the years, the city has been a little lenient on the ordinance under certain circumstances. I had no problem with that because times change, but the ordinance was on the books and enforceable when necessary. Sometimes people change and are not so wild, which makes a difference in how you govern, plus the drinking age was raised back to 21 a few years later.

Mrs. Louise Karn may have been disqualified to run for mayor of Evanston, but it had just been announced in the Uinta County Herald that she had been temporarily appointed as Justice of the Peace. She would hold the position until the next election, which would be in November of 1976. It was also announced that UHF Community TV would be discontinued on December 10th, but shortly afterwards an announcement came out that Western TV would keep the UHF system on the air along with the cable TV system. This made a lot of folks happy and appreciative of former Mayor Bob Burns. It was a great move by Burns.

1975 was a year to remember with all the controversy going on, but it felt good to get some of those things off our minds, especially the Cowboy Days problem. I thought, for his first year, that Mayor South had done a good job. I felt he had been fair and honest on all issues. I knew that the next few years were going to be just as tough, but I felt good about the mayor and thought that he would be very capable of handling what would be ahead of us. And, we hoped that the "open container ordinance" would help control the wild crowds during Cowboy Days and other special events.

CHAPTER 10

1976.... 1976 started off with a controversial issue during the first general meeting of the city council on January 5th. The problem was between Evanston's Chief of Police David Schrader, Justice of the Peace Louise Karn, and County Attorney Chuck Phillips. Mrs. Karn had been appointed recently by the Uinta County Commissioners to act as the Justice of the Peace until the next election which would be in November of this year. Karn would be replacing the previous judge, Roy Matthews, who had passed away the past year.

There was some concern about a court case in December at which Chief Schrader was scheduled to be present, but he never appeared. Because of his absence, County Attorney Phillips and Judge Karn decided that he should be reprimanded.

Chief Schrader stated that this particular incident was a build-up of circumstances and that he was only made aware that his testimony might be needed only the day before. He said his understanding was that arrangements were being made so that he wouldn't be needed. He also said that he felt this was an isolated case and that he didn't mean to be disrespectful to any court. The reprimand was dismissed.

However, during this meeting, Mayor South requested that Chief Schrader attend the meeting with the county concerning the new county jail, in the planning stage at that time. Again, the chief did not attend the meeting. County Commissioner Richard Sims was also at the meeting and said that he thought the city should have had some representation from the Evanston Police Department to be able to present any suggestions that they may have. He said he thought this new jail should be a joint project between the communities and the county, and that he would like more communication between City and County Law Enforcement concerning the new facility. Mayor South agreed.

Chief Schrader also reported that burglaries were getting to be a real problem. He said that lately we had three burglaries: at the Outpost Restaurant, the Western TV store and the Eagles Club. He said that the only solutions to the matter would be to remind businesses to make sure their establishments were well secured and that we have our officers patrolling the areas a little more often. But, he pointed out that they were already spread out quite a bit.

1976 would be the year of the country's Bicentennial of the American Revolution. A committee would be formed to plan various programs throughout the year, especially on the 4th of July. This would also be the Year of the Dragon for Chinese New Year, which we would celebrate on January 30th and 31st. This year's program would be co-chaired by Denice Wheeler and Ralph Stock.

During the meeting, City Engineer John Proffit reported on the sewage disposal plant. He stated that all of the flow is going through the plant at the present time, and no raw sewage was going into the river. He said parts had been ordered for the needed repairs and should be on hand soon. He also stated that Fay Riebennacht was doing a good job keeping the ice broken up and keeping the plant in good operation.

Other business during the January meeting was two resignations. We received the resignation of Ted Ellingford, City Attorney. Ellingford hadn't been with the city very long, but he was going into construction and was going to quit law entirely. We also received the resignation of Officer Jake Williams. Both resignations were accepted with sorrow and regret, and now we would be without an attorney once again. The mayor and council thanked them both for their past service and wished them well for the future. Bruce Waters was accepted and hired as a new police officer, and I reported that the Governor's Crime Commission, which I was appointed to along with County Commissioner Gene Taylor, would meet in Evanston January 15th and that anyone with interest was invited to attend.

As president of the Greater Evanston Development Company, I gave a report to the council that we had our meeting and the new directors were me, Rudy Ellingford, Blaine Sanders, Ralph Elardi,

Wilford Lym, Sam Hart and Tony Martin, and that we would be meeting in February to elect new officers. I also reported that we now had 56 stockholders who held a total of 5,056 shares. Anyone interested in buying shares could purchase them at $1.00 per share, and anyone would be welcome to participate. However, by S.B.A. regulations, no one could hold a controlling interest. It was a non-profit corporation. The sole purpose of the company was to build industry and encourage new business by helping find funding for them.

During the regular council meeting on February 3rd, Attorney James H. Phillips accepted the position of city attorney, replacing Ted Ellingford, and was sworn in by City Clerk Don Welling. Also present was Mr. Woody Russell from the Wyoming Department of Environmental Quality. He was there to remind the city council about burning at the city dumps. He reminded the council that it was illegal and that we must stop or we could be facing a sizeable penalty or fine.

Mayor South thanked Russell for being present and for once again reminding us of the problem, and the mayor assured him that we were very much aware of the situation. He told Russell that we were in the process of trying to locate property that can be used as a landfill.

Mayor South also informed the council that he would be accompanying John Proffit and James Phillips to a meeting in Cheyenne to meet with the Wyoming Farm Loan Board and another agency to see about getting a grant to help with our water and sewer problems. Evanston and the town of Lyman were both told that there would be no funds available at this time, but to apply again at a later date. Both communities were badly in need of some help with their water and sewer problems.

The Wyoming Farm Loan Board was made up of Wyoming's top five elected officials: the Governor, the Secretary of State, the State Auditor, the State Treasurer and the State Superintendent of Public Instruction. The board had full control of all state-owned lands, and at that particular meeting Mayor South mentioned the possibility of leasing some state land for a landfill. He informed the board that Evanston was still burning at our city dumps. He also told them that the Wyoming Department of Environmental Quality had warned us that we had to stop, and that we had to find a new location for a landfill.

Other business that came up during the meeting was the acceptance of various subdivisions, easements and right-of-ways. Kennedy, Public Works Director, requested some new equipment and permission to trim some trees that were interfering with parking. Both requests were approved and Chief Schrader gave his police report.

Mr. Bollschweiler was present once again, reminding the council of their water rights throughout the city, and County Commissioner Gene Martin was in attendance to inform the council of the proposed additional one cent sales tax. He stated that it was very important that we get this on the ballot for the election and, if passed, Evanston would benefit very much from it. He said in order to get this on the ballot for the election they would need at least 10% of qualified voters from the county to sign a petition. The mayor thanked Martin for taking the initiative in getting these signatures and said that he believed that all members of the council were in favor and would be willing to sign the petition.

The Greater Evanston Development Company held their February meeting and, once again, I was re-elected as president. There wasn't much change in any of the offices, but the usual discussion was held on how to entice new industry and businesses to the area to create new jobs.

About that time an article came out in the Uinta County Herald titled AMOCO REPORTS SUCCESSFUL WELL and that on February 12, 1976 the Amoco Production Company had successfully tested a wildcat well in Southwest Wyoming. Amoco Vice President and Denver Division Manager James W. Vanderbeek made the announcement. The discovery was a gas well that flowed at the rate of 5.8 million cubic feet per day along with a spray of condensate during one test. Production was encountered in the Nugget formation at a depth of 7,445 feet. This discovery was the first of many gas wells that would create the largest oil and gas boom in the history of Evanston, and possibly in the State of Wyoming.

The well was located about 14 miles northeast of Evanston in an area known as the Overthrust Belt and was on Union Pacific Railroad property leased to Amoco. The well was operated by Amoco, but both the Chevron Oil Company and the Champlin Petroleum Company (Champlin is the oil company of the Union Pacific Railroad Corp.) had shares in the well. Since that big discovery northeast of town, the Evanston area became a hot spot for oil and gas production as reported by the Uinta County Herald. The February 19th headline read, EVANSTON IS OIL "HOT SPOT". For the past year or so there had been a lot of seismographic activity going on in the area and several independent oil and gas brokers had bought up mineral leases on all the properties available, including those within the city limits of Evanston.

Through the seismograph activities, it was discovered that there was oil under the City of Evanston. One of the oil brokers from Denver named Hal McVey was trying to buy up all the mineral leases he could by going house to house and meeting with the Evanston Chamber of Commerce. He was soliciting all owners within the city who held mineral rights on their property. He explained that the three big oil companies, Amoco, Chevron and Champlin, would be doing some directional drilling under the city and everyone that owned the mineral rights on their property would be receiving royalties, but if the railroad or any previous owner retained the mineral rights the property owner would not receive any royalties.

Mr. McVey assured the membership that any drilling under the town would be done by directional drilling from oil well rigs set up outside of the city limits.

However, before the oil boom was over we had as many as twelve oil rigs set up within the limits of the city. He also expressed concern over the discoveries of gas and oil in the outer areas of Evanston and warned us of a population boom, suggesting that we should begin to prepare for it, to be ready if and when it occurred. He stated that in addition to the top three oil companies there would be others as well, such as Gulf Oil Corporation.

After listening to McVey and other representatives from the oil industry, Mayor South called for a special meeting for the following

Tuesday, February 24th to discuss the leasing of city property to an oil company. But first he directed City Attorney Phillips to draw up a lease agreement and a bid proposal and issue them to all potential bidders to be used for preparing their bids. It was said that the city could receive as much as $40,000 to $60,000 for mineral leases of its lands, plus .12½ per cent or more in royalty benefits from the gas and oil extracted. It was suggested by the representatives that a five-year lease would likely be a minimum length for them.

County and city officials in southwestern Wyoming had been studying, for some time, ways to prepare for a population boom. The experience of our neighboring towns and cities such as Lyman, Green River and Rock Springs offered some advice and assistance gained from their experiences during their more recent boom, which had been caused by the increase in production and additional mining of the trona industry located in Sweetwater County. The impact from that boom hit the Bridger Valley area as hard as it hit the communities in the neighboring county. Evanston had experienced small boom scares in the past, but many of the old-timers in Evanston felt that this boom was going to be the biggest yet and would materialize into something for real. It did.

Many of the citizens had expressed concern about leasing mineral rights under their properties. City officials were also concerned and somewhat uncertain. The mayor told the citizens that the city would be exploring the issue very carefully before their regular meeting on March 2nd. This was an indication of the importance of the upcoming vote on the passage of the additional one cent sales tax increase. Although it would probably be a year or two before we would see any benefits from it, it would be something that would be of a big help when we did start receiving it.

During the regular meeting of the city council on March 2nd, there was one bid received to update and repair the sewage treatment plant to meet E.P.A. standards, from T.J.G. Corporation in the amount of $7,458. Also, a bid for an alarm system at the plant to be hooked up in case of high water was awarded to Cazin's in the amount of $250. Both bids were accepted with all voting in favor.

Mr. Phillips, City Attorney, brought up the idea of forming a Housing Authority and explained how this could benefit the city, but he said we had to apply immediately and have the application in the hands of the General Powers of Municipalities Community Housing Authority by March 9th. The council decided they would wait on this project, but would keep it in mind.

Mr. Phil Mensing, who was overseeing and running the projector at the Strand Theatre, requested the right to show the movie "Deep Throat" at the Strand. The movie at that time was very controversial. It was considered to have pornographic scenes that weren't appropriate for public viewing. Mayor South said he would contact Mr. Ken Hiatt, owner of the theatre, requesting this film not to be shown in Evanston, and it never was.

During the meeting there was more discussion on street lights, requests for more bids and general public works issues, and there were a few appointments made to various boards and committees. There was also more discussion about a landfill and possible sites were mentioned. The question of leasing the mineral rights under city-owned property was scheduled for a special meeting to be held on March 9th.

On March 9th the special meeting was held and sealed bids were opened. Although bid packages were sent out to several oil and interested parties, we only received three sealed bids back. The bids received were from the Gulf Oil Company, Hal A. McVey and Burton-Hawks, Inc. After the bids were opened and after a considerable amount of discussion, the Evanston City Council accepted the highest bid, which was from Burton-Hawks. In their bid they offered a payment of $225.00 per acre, plus 20% royalty on minerals extracted. The life of the lease was five years. At that time, the city had mineral rights on approximately 215 acres, which were included in the bid. This gave the city a total of $48,375 to be paid immediately upon the final acceptance of the bid. Any royalties received would be based only on how much, if any, oil and gas was actually produced under the lands.

Other business at the meeting included Chief Schrader submitting his letter of resignation effective as of May 31st. He stated that he was getting out of police work and had another job offer in Evanston that was not related to law enforcement. I had the idea that he was just getting tired of the politics involved with being chief. Mayor South and the council accepted his resignation with some regret, because we felt that he had done a fairly good job, especially in organizing the reserve unit and handling the Cowboy Days situation.

At our regular meeting of April 2nd, we had the usual business such as liquor license renewals, bid openings and the four days that the liquor dealers were allowed to stay open 24 hours. This was allowed by state law and was usually requested by the liquor dealers early each year.

Although Chief Schrader had resigned as of May 31st, he was at the meeting to give his report on the police activity for the prior month. During his report he also read a letter of resignation from Officer Randall Martin, effective April 15th. The mayor and council accepted his resignation and told the chief to tell him thanks for his service and that we all wished him well.

City Engineer John Proffit told of a meeting that he and City Attorney James Phillips had attended in Cheyenne with the Wyoming Community Development Authority and the Wyoming Farm Loan Board. Proffit said that evidently the W.C.D.A. hadn't followed proper procedure to obtain funds, and that the Farm Loan Board would not advance any money to them until they had all their requirements and procedures in proper order.

Ordinance #314 was introduced by Councilman Dawson to establish that all regular meetings of the Evanston City Council shall be conducted on the first Wednesday after the first Tuesday of each and every month, commencing May 5, 1976, and shall begin at 5:00 p.m. Councilman Davis made the motion to suspend the rules and deal with this ordinance as an emergency, seconded by Council Fife. The motion passed with all voting in favor.

After Ordinance #314 was read by title a motion was made by Fife, seconded by Dawson, and the motion passed with all voting in favor. The change in our regular meeting schedule was because there was getting to be so much business that our meetings ran much later.

The mayor and council felt that it would be best to start the meetings earlier in the day and later in the month, giving city officials more time to prepare for the meeting. The regular meetings had been on the first Tuesday of the month and began at 7:00 p.m. Sometimes the first Tuesday would fall on the first or second day of the month, which wouldn't give the clerk and others very much time to prepare for the meeting.

During the meeting Mayor South announced that there would be a special meeting to be held at the Uinta County Court House on April 6th at 7:00 p.m. The meeting would be with representatives from the oil companies and construction companies and any others interested in current developments in the city. Also, Mayor South called for another special meeting of the council and city officials on April 8th at 7:00 p.m. to discuss the garbage and sanitation problem further.

Also in April's regular meeting, Mr. Robert Lowham and Mr. Douglas Ellsworth, representing the Masonic Cemetery Association, asked the council if the city would be interested in taking care of the Masonic Cemetery for the next year for a fee. A fee was discussed, but Allen Kennedy, General Foreman of Public Works, was directed to look into the number of plots and the work this would involve and come up with a fair fee.

The special meeting that Mayor South called for on April 6th at the Uinta County Court House was packed. A number of oil and gas representatives were on hand, as well as representatives from the coal industry and the utility companies. There was also a large number of local citizens in attendance. During the discussion there were many questions asked, but the representatives from the oil and gas industry played down the impact and didn't think we were going to have the growth in population that we were expecting. Boy, were they ever wrong.

At the special meeting on April 8th, Councilman Dawson presented a proposed garbage contract for the council's consideration. The proposal would come under advisory at a later date. Plans were to start on the new sanitary landfill with some temporary arrangements at the new site and covering up of the old dump. The new landfill would be located about a mile east of the old dump. The property would belong to the State of Wyoming and the city would lease approximately 60 acres for the landfill, but it would be a while before it would be ready for use. In the meantime, the old dumps would still be used. Mayor South told the council that he would approach the county for some help with equipment and some manpower, and we needed to get started on this right away.

That spring the City of Evanston received a congratulatory letter from the United States Environmental Protection Agency on its excellent operation of the Evanston sewage treatment plant. The letter was received by the plant operator, Mr. Riebennacht.

Although the Wyoming Railway Car Corporation was doing very well and business was up and I felt good about helping to bring the company to Evanston, I wasn't too pleased with some things that were going on. I confronted Colonel Shiflet about it, but he didn't want to make any changes. I just didn't feel right about the backstabbing and some of the more unethical things that were happening. I don't think anything that was going on was illegal, but I felt that the Colonel was doing a few things that were very unethical and I didn't want to be a part of it, so I quit the job after having a short talk with Shiflet.

Although I didn't approve of some of the things going on at the plant, I still had a lot of respect for the Colonel. He was very intelligent and a great promoter. I was damn glad that he came to Evanston and got the plant going. At this time he had approximately 50 employees working for him. He was also very goodhearted; a person couldn't help but like him, but he didn't always tell the truth, and that bothered me.

Another special council meeting was called by Mayor South on April 12th at 5:00 p.m. The purpose of the meeting was to pass a resolution that would allow the City of Evanston to enter into a Joint Powers Agreement with the County of Uinta, State of Wyoming, to create a Joint Powers Board to apply for grants and loans in a more effective way to receive funding for our water supply transmission and distribution system. Councilman Dawson moved for the adoption of the resolution, seconded by Fife, with all voting in favor.

It wasn't too long after the Joint Powers Board was formed that Evanston received a loan from the Wyoming Farm Loan Board in the amount of $1,035,000 to help upgrade our water systems, eventually eliminating the problem of having to ration water every year.

Also at this meeting Officer Mel Wren, a member of the Evanston Police Department, was appointed to the position of Acting Chief of Police, replacing David Schrader. He stated that he would be making only a few changes in the department at this time, but later on there may be more. He thanked the mayor and council and hoped that he could make them proud of him.

Another special council meeting was called for April 23rd at 12:15 p.m. to pass a resolution to execute an oil and gas lease between the City of Evanston and Burton-Hawks, Inc., releasing all mineral rights presently owned by the city. I moved for the adoption of the resolution, seconded by Councilman Lunsford. The motion passed with all voting in favor. Mr. Bruce Studer, representing Burton-Hawks, presented Mayor South with a draft in the amount of $1,119.38 for approximately five acres of additional land.

May 18, 1976 was the date set for the election of the additional 1% sales tax. All of this tax would remain within the county and its cities and towns for local government use. This increase would make the sales tax in Uinta County 4% instead of the 3% that had been the amount of sales tax set by the State of Wyoming for many years.

Mayor South stated that passage of the sales tax proposal was essential to the City of Evanston if services were to be maintained and increased to meet growing demands. He encouraged everyone to vote to accept the tax proposal, because two years ago it was denied, leaving the county and communities in a bad position at a time when more revenue was in dire need.

The first regular meeting to follow on a Wednesday, on May 5th, had a full agenda with several resolutions, and subdivisions and general business concerning the various problems of a number of citizens. The meeting was called to order at 5:00 p.m. by Mayor South with the minutes of previous meetings and the payment of bills being approved by motion and seconded with all voting in favor.

Jerry Wall, a member of the recreation board, was at the meeting to present to the council a plan for a recreation district. The plan would involve a joint school-city-county program with a full-time supervisor. She explained that under present law a one mill levy could be collected through the county to go towards recreation by forming a recreation district that would be made up of a nine member control board. A discussion followed and most thought it sounded like a good idea, but in the meantime the Evanston Recreation Board would remain unchanged. However, this would be something the board would discuss at a later time.

Margaret Smith, whose residence was on County Road, approached the mayor and city council, a little angry about the garbage problem in her neighborhood. She stated that it was getting worse and she thought that the city should make an effort to get it cleaned up. Mayor South instructed Acting Chief Mel Wren and Allen Kennedy, General Foreman of Public Works, to investigate the complaint and report back to the mayor.

However, her problem apparently didn't get taken care of, because that wasn't the last we heard from her. Miss Smith had recently retired from the U.S. Army and had never been married. She had moved back to Evanston and moved into her parent's old home after their death. Smith, being an old army gal, had one hell of a temper and when she got mad she didn't give a damn who was around, and she had a mouth on her that would make a muleskinner sound like a saint, and she had no problem using the big "F" word.

It was unbelievable, how this problem ended. It was probably the most unexpected and the strangest incident that I had ever witnessed while serving on the council. I don't know whether Chief Wren or Allen Kennedy ever got back to the mayor or not. Probably not, because at the next meeting, Miss Smith arrived with a black garbage bag that appeared to be full, and set it down in front of her. No one paid much attention to that, but when the mayor called on her to express her problem, she stood up, grabbed that bag, walked up to the council bench towards the mayor, and turned the bag upside down, emptying it on the bench right in front of the mayor and said, *There's your f------ garbage that I gathered up in our f------ neighborhood."* I'll never forget those words. The mayor was really shaken up. He moved his chair back away from the bench trying to keep the garbage off of him, but he was so dumbfounded that he didn't know what to say. But Miss Smith sure knew what to say because she just kept ranting on with that hard core language for a few more minutes and then left. I believe the entire council was not only taken by surprise, but embarrassed and all shook up, and I believe the visitors were likewise.

She finally left, but she got the attention she needed, because after that the neighborhood was kept pretty clean and we never heard from her again. I believe she was pleased with the area after that, but she sure let us know that she was back in town and we had better listen.

During that same meeting on May 5th, reports were made on the landfill, on the police department and the police reserve. New subdivisions were presented and handled accordingly, and several residences outside the city limits requested the city's permission to hook up to city water and sewer. It was stated by the attorney that he would look into the legalities concerning the out-of-city hookups and check to see if other communities in the state were allowing this and what fees they were charging.

City Engineer Proffit stated that at this time he would be opposed to any hookups outside the city limits until the area was annexed because of the difficulty in securing easements and controlling future hookups. A lengthy discussion followed in which many problems were mentioned and the matter was tabled for the present time.

Patsy Madia, representing the Uinta County Senior Citizens, told the council that the Methodist Association had agreed to sell the Church, located on the corner of 10th Street and Center, where they were presently leasing and wondered if the city could help acquire funds to assist Uinta County in purchasing the building for a senior citizen center. The council told her that they would consider the request but that a lot would depend on the passage of the continuance of the 1% sales tax, which was once again coming up for re-election by the citizens of Uinta County.

Representatives from the Superior Fire Apparatus Company talked to the council about entering into a contract with them to purchase a Superior Pumper, Booster, and an Arial Ladder Apparatus for the fire department. As this would be on contract, it would have to be approved by a resolution. After some discussion Councilman Lunsford made a motion to adopt the resolution, seconded by Dawson. The motion passed with all voting in favor. Lunsford reminded the council that 10% of the total price of the fire equipment would have to be paid up front as a down payment, and would be paid for out of Revenue Sharing Funds.

At the end of the meeting, Mr. Proffit explained that the loan and grant money received from W.C.D.A. and the Farm Loan Board was made available to the city for a water development project. He also explained that there will be a need in the near future for new sewer lines in some of the areas of the city. He also mentioned that some lines were getting old and would need to be replaced eventually.

Acting Chief Wren announced that he had lost some of his police reserve, but had recruited others. At the present, he said, we now had in his reserve program Forrest Bright, Tom Marshall, J. R. Dean, Bob Pasenelli, Frank Maioran, Barry Rochford, Craig Nelson, Lora Jones, Joe Fessenden, Bob and Billie Pryor, Phil Mensing and Sonny Blakeslee. He mentioned that all these members had either already been through the police training program or were going through it at the present.

Wren also mentioned that the new jail contract went to Newland Construction Company, a local contractor. Newland's low bid was for $464,000 with the next lowest bid from L. M. Olsen Construction Company of Rawlins, Wyoming, for $481,000. He stated that construction would start immediately.

After quitting the Railway Car Company I had no idea what I would be doing next, but one day I was talking to Otto Kennedy, a former partner in the truck stop and a good friend. In our conversation he suggested that I go into real estate. I thought about it and talked to one of my old Jaycee associates from Jackson who was a real estate broker. He also encouraged the idea.

Then I visited with Elaine Blakeslee (Michaelis), one of the owners of Uinta Title and Insurance Company and Uinta Realty, and one of the few real estate brokers in Evanston. She said she would be willing to sponsor me so I could apply for a salesman's license. You couldn't become a real estate salesman unless you had a broker willing to sponsor you. You had to work under a broker for at least two years before you yourself could become a broker, and in addition you had to have some schooling.

I also thought about selling insurance, so I talked to Percy Hudson who was selling for Franklin Life Insurance at the time. He said he would be more than happy to sponsor me so I could also take the insurance examination to get my insurance license and work under him.

I passed the exam for both the real estate and the insurance licenses and immediately went to work trying to sell real estate and insurance. There wasn't much real estate listed for sale in Evanston at the time so I spent most of my time in Bridger Valley where there was a lot of real estate for sale because of the trona boom in Sweetwater County. I spent nine months selling real estate before I made a sale and received a commission check.

While selling insurance I sold a few life insurance policies, but I didn't care much for it because I didn't feel good about trying to sell something that wasn't material, or something that you could see and put your hands on and use it immediately. Real estate was different because it was real property and buildings that were actually visible, so I felt much better trying to sell something that you could see rather than just a piece of paper to look at. I didn't stay in the insurance business very long, but I did stay with real estate, and in a couple years I got my broker's license and took over Uinta Realty from Blakeslee because she didn't want to have anything to do with selling real estate. She eventually ended up owning the Uinta Title and Insurance Company after buying her partners out.

Elaine Blakeslee was a good lady, one of the hardest-working people I have ever known, and she was good to work for because you knew just where you stood. She didn't put up with any nonsense, and she expected a lot from her employees. She was very successful, and later, as a widow, she continued to operate the business the same as she always had. She was a good hardworking and honest person, and she was very successful. I considered her one of my best friends.

That same summer I met with Rick Sather who owned a store on Main Street between 11th and 12th Streets where the post office is now located. He talked to me about opening up a sporting goods store in his building. I considered the idea and talked to my wife Sandy about it. We agreed to give it a try and have our third son, Tib, operate it. So I met with Mr. Bradbury at the First National Bank to request a loan. He actually tried to talk me out of it, claiming that no one had ever been successful in the sporting goods business, mainly because of the tough competition in Salt Lake City. But after talking to him about it and telling him that I thought I could make it work he gave in and gave me the loan I needed to open the store.

So now I was selling real estate and trying to operate a sporting goods store with the help of Sandy and our son, Tib. The store offered mostly camping and hunting supplies, including guns, but we did sell some athletic equipment and sometimes I would sell some sporting supplies to the schools in Evanston and Bridger Valley.

A special meeting was called by Mayor South in late May to talk with the Planning and Zoning Commission about some changes in the zoning ordinance, and the issue of business licenses came up. Apparently, there were a lot of businesses that were operating with no license. At this time the city attorney, James Phillips, was directed by the mayor to look into the changes that were discussed concerning the zoning ordinance and to check on our ordinance concerning business licenses. Because of the growth, it seemed that we were amending the zoning ordinance quite often. I guess we were just trying to keep up with the times.

The election on the 1% increase in sales tax was held, and a school bond issue was also on the ballot, with both issues passing by a large margin. The council was very happy about this, but it would be another year before the city and county would benefit. It was something to look forward to in planning our future budgets.

The regular meeting of June 2nd was postponed until June 15th at 5:00 p.m. because of not having a quorum. For various reasons there were only two council members present at the regular meeting: Lowell Dawson and me; therefore the meeting was postponed.

The City of Evanston requested that the Federal Government Census Bureau take a current census of Evanston, because we felt that since 1970, the last census taken had shown a far lower population than what the present would show. They recently took a census for the town of Lyman and it showed an increase from 643 in 1970 to 2002 in 1976. One main reason for the request was that state funds from sales tax collections and other state moneys were distributed by population and at this time the City of Evanston and Uinta County were getting shortchanged; however, at that time the city and county both signed acceptance of the population count of Lyman to show goodwill.

At the June 15th meeting we also discussed the use and sale of fireworks in the city limits. Fire Chief Jerry Cazin reviewed portions of the City Ordinance 291 which prohibits the use and manufacturing of fireworks. I read a portion of the ordinance which stated, *It shall be unlawful for any person to store, offer for sale, expose for sale, sell at retail for use, or explode any fireworks except as provided in Section 13.3c through 13.3f.*

The section referred to allowed public displays controlled by various organizations such as the Jaycees who have conducted the display in the past for the 4th of July celebration, which required a special permit. Chief Cazin requested permission to publish an article in the next issue of the Uinta County Herald concerning the fireworks ordinance. Mayor South, with council approval, stated that just before the holiday would be a good time.

At that time no business was permitted to sell fireworks within the city limits, plus it was against the law to even use them in the city except for special use authorized by permit. However, there was one business just outside the city limits that sold them because there was no law against selling or using them in the state or county. Therefore, most of the fireworks that the locals used were let off outside of the city limits, and a lot of Utah folks came to Wyoming to buy fire-works, because they were illegal in Utah statewide.

It was election year, and at the meeting Don Welling, City Clerk, announced that the filing dates were a little different this year. He said the dates would be from July 19th to August 4th, which was about a month later than in the past, and that filing forms would be available at the clerk's office. He also stated that the three council members who would be up for re-election would be Jon Lunsford, Ward 1; Melvin Baldwin, Ward 2; and Roger Fife, Ward 3.

Hal McVey, representing one of the oil companies, was back in town that summer still trying to buy oil and gas leases from residential and business owners. He made a visit to our home and gave us a fair offer on two pieces of property that we had owned and had the mineral rights on. It was about another year before we started seeing anything out of it, but we did end up getting some royalties for the next four or five years from the oil that was extracted from under the city by directional drilling. It was kind of neat to know you were receiving royalties for your mineral rights, but it wasn't something that was going to make you rich, when you were only receiving a few dollars every once in a while.

At the regular council meeting of July 7th we acted on the third and final reading of the Guild Subdivision and allowed Mr. Guild to immediately start selling lots in the subdivision. Previously he had requested permission to begin selling lots prior to the third and final reading of the ordinance, but City Attorney Phillips warned against it because if things didn't go right it could cause some serious problems. Therefore, in the past, the city council denied his request.

Mel Wren, Acting Chief of Police, reported that they were having problems at Hamblin Park. He said there had been late parties going on and that a lot of vandalism had occurred. He said the police had been called to break up these parties and they had made some arrests, but had not been able to prevent the vandalism. He said that the department would make an effort to patrol the park more often.

Mayor South expressed his appreciation for the police department and suggested that Wren be appointed as Chief of Police. The council members all concurred with the decision. Motion was made by Councilman Dawson, and seconded by me with all voting in favor. Wren was no longer just acting as chief, he was now officially appointed, confirmed, and sworn in as Chief of Police.

Filing dates for those wishing to run for office were now open. Russell "Bub" Albrecht from Ward 1 was the first to file for city council. Councilman Dawson announced that he would not finish out his term and that he would be resigning soon so that the council could appoint someone to fill the vacant seat in Ward 2 that he would leave. The appointment would only be for the rest of the year. Someone from Ward 2 would have to run for the two years remaining of Dawson's term. This was also a presidential election year. Vice President Gerald Ford, who became president after the resignation of President Richard Nixon, ran for president against Governor Jimmy Carter of Georgia.

At our regular meeting of August 4th, City Engineer Proffit gave a report on the water improvement project. The Wyoming Farm Loan Board was ready to fund the project as soon as the city was able to furnish the collateral necessary, easements, and so on. After a lengthy discussion the council agreed to go ahead with the project as soon as possible.

Some sewer problems were also discussed. Since the city had adopted the state uniform plumbing code, all restaurants, cafés, vehicle repair garages and service stations were required to have installed grease traps to avoid plugged sewer lines. More subdivision plats were presented and approved. Two, the Sage Industrial Park and the Hartzell Estate Subdivision, were presented by Charles Albrecht. Both were approved and accepted by the council.

A letter of resignation from Councilman Lowell Dawson was read by the mayor. Dawson was moving out of Evanston. Motion was made by me and seconded by Lunsford to accept his resignation with regrets and a statement that he would be missed. The motion passed, followed by comments from the mayor expressing his sorrow but wishing him well and thanking him for his service.

The mayor said that we should appoint someone to replace him immediately, and suggested that Mr. Rees "Tubb" Nichols be appointed to the council to fill the vacancy. It was moved by me and seconded by Lunsford to appoint Nichols immediately to fill the vacancy. The motion passed with all voting in favor.

Other business was a new appointment to the Planning and Zoning Commission. Mr. Larry Holmes had resigned, and with Councilman Baldwin's recommendation, Mr. Rudy Ellingford was appointed by motion to fulfill Holmes's vacancy.

Chief Wren gave his report concerning the Evanston Cowboy Days celebration, stating that it went off a lot smoother than the previous years. He said, *Cowboy Days was a busy weekend for the city, although it was more enjoyable than in the past years. This is a great comeback for the city and I hope that the future years of Cowboy Days continues in this manner,* he added.

He said that there was a good turnout of families, locals and outsiders, and that everyone seemed to enjoy themselves. He stated that they had some problems, but nothing like they had the previous years, thanks to the new Open Container Ordinance. He also expressed his appreciation to all the law enforcement officers that helped keep the event running smoothly, and thanked the bar operators for their cooperation and assistance in reminding their patrons about the new ordinance. The mayor and council then commended Chief Wren and his department for their efforts in controlling the weekend.

Bernard C. Gram was honored for his services as the Civil Defense Coordinator and for the cooperation and services he had provided to the National Guard. Wyoming Adjutant General James Spence from Cheyenne was on hand to make the presentation to Gram by honoring him with the Outstanding Citizen's Award, an honor well deserved.

It was also reported at that time that the school enrollment was up 4½% over last year. This was an indication that our population was growing, and we needed to continue upgrading our infrastructure to keep up with it.

Engineer Proffit reported that the water project was coming along fine and that plans for running water lines and installation of storage tanks were being made, and easements were being obtained where needed.

I announced that the Wyoming Recreation Commission had called me concerning the tennis court, wondering what our plans were. Councilman Fife suggested that we remove the old courts and apply for a grant to build two new courts. With the council all agreeing to the suggestion, I was directed to relate our plans to the Wyoming commission.

Other projects discussed were subdivision, roadways, easements, downtown parking and the water intake located on the upper Bear River near the Myers Ranch. Brent Bergen, representing the Senior Citizens, explained their plans for the improvement of the old Methodist church building that the seniors had recently purchased.

It was also announced that the Primary Election would be held on September 14th and that everyone should make an effort to vote. Those running for city council were: for Ward 1, Russel "Bub" Albrecht, Bruce R. Heyborne and Jerry Wall; for Ward 2, Phil Peterson and Jimmie Rice. These were for the 4-year term. Those running for the 2-year term in Ward 2 were Jeffery Carlton, Richard Deen and Roy Fruits. Rees "Tubb" Nichols did not wish to run for the position he was holding because of the resignation of Lowell Dawson. Running in Ward 3 would be Roger Fife, David Bills and Marvin Bollschweiler. A problem came up with the Planning and Zoning Commission when a Mr. Charles Alexander made a request to build another apartment house on property that he owned on the corner of 9th Street and Summit Street where he already had a fourplex being rented. He had enough space on the property to put another building and he could meet the legal setbacks and have adequate parking, but the building would be a six apartment building and would be built so close to the home of Mrs. Maude Morgan and would be so high that it would overshadow her home and she would get no sunshine.

Mrs. Morgan met with the board with her objections to the structure. She had stated that she had lived there for many years and that her children had all been raised there. She went on to remind the council that the property was zoned for single family homes only, and the height of the building would block all the sunshine from the southwest that they had enjoyed so much over the years.

There was a lot of opposition against Mr. Alexander's request considering all the letters received from the public by the board and the city. After considerable discussion, the P & Z Commission sent a "do not pass" recommendation to the mayor and council. I was one of the council members involved with the commission and I agreed with them. Their main reasons were that the property was not zoned for multiple housing, they felt that it would set a precedent, and they were taking into account all the opposition. The recommendation was sent to the city council to take final action.

With all the discussion and concern shown by so many people, Mayor South said that we had better invite Mr. Alexander to our next meeting. Mr. Harry Lee Harris, Alexander's attorney, stated that he would send a request to Mr. Alexander to be at the next meeting. Although Alexander had not lived in Evanston for many years, he was born and raised here and he knew a lot of the local folks, so he did have some support in what he was trying to do.

At the next meeting Alexander showed up with his attorney, Harry Lee Harris, a native of Evanston and a local lawyer. The subject was put on the floor by Mayor South, who was in favor of Alexander's request. Discussion was long and lengthy. I knew Alexander very well and considered him as a friend, and I had also been in the army with him, but I knew what Mrs. Morgan was up against and I knew she was right. Therefore, I spoke against Alexander's request. I told the council that it would set a precedent when others applied for similar zone changes, but most of all I felt bad for Mrs. Morgan. I went on to say that because of how close the building would be to her house and because of the height, it would shadow her home allowing no sunshine. And, I stated, there's not a one of you that wouldn't feel the same as Mrs. Morgan if it was your home. However, after all the discussion and arguing the council made a motion to accept Mr. Alexander's request with 4 ayes and 2 nays. I don't recall who the other nay was, but I was one of them.

After the decision was made concerning the Alexander apartment complex, the Uinta County Herald published a news article that was titled PLANNING COMMISSION DISAPPROVES OF ACTION

OF EVANSTON CITY COUNCIL, stating how the P & Z Commission felt about the city's decision. The article went on to print the letter in full, as follows:

> *The Evanston Planning and Zoning Commission would like to inform the people of Evanston that the Planning and Zoning Commission is in total opposition to the construction of the Alexander 6-plex on part of Lots 8, 9 and 10 of Block 13 of the Original Town of Evanston.*

The letter went on to say, *The Planning and Zoning Commission has on several occasions reviewed the Alexander request to construct a building on the above mentioned property and has denied the request because it was in violation of several sections of Ordinance 286 and against the wishes of the surrounding property owners. After our most recent denial on December 5, 1975, we were informed that although the Rules of Practice for the Planning and Zoning Commission had been adopted, and the record of the action can be found in Planning and Zoning Commission minutes of January 17, 1972; the Rules of Practice were not then filed with the Secretary of State as required by the Wyoming Administrative Procedures Act. According to that act, 'no agency, rule, order or decision is valid or effective against any person or property, or may it be invoked by the agency until it has been made available for public inspection as herein required'. The "Public Inspector" referred to has been interpreted as being filed with the office of the Secretary of State. Due to the above mentioned act, our ruling regarding the Alexander request was declared null and void.* The letter went on to say, *Because of the legal technicality, the City Council was advised by the City Attorney that they should rule in favor of the construction of the Alexander building.*

And finally it said, *The Planning and Zoning Commission strongly disapproves of the action taken by the Council.*

That was the entire letter sent to the newspaper to be printed and I for one agree wholeheartedly with it. I felt that the council had made a big mistake. The apartment is still standing to this day and still shading the house next door that Mrs. Morgan lived in. I believe the motion made by the council caused that house to lose a lot of value.

Planning Commission Disapproves Of Action Of Evanston City Council

At a special meeting Monday, October 25th, the members of the Evanston Planning and Zoning Commission expressed opposition to the ruling of the City Council concerning the approval of request for Charles Alexander to construct a six-unit apartment house.

The Commission issued a statement concerning the action which fully explains their position. We are pleased to print it in full below.

"The Evanston Planning and Zoning Commission would like to inform the people of the City of Evanston, that the Planning and Zoning Commission is in total opposition to the construction of the Alexander 6-plex on part of Lots 8, 9 and 10 of Block 33, of the Original Town of Evanston.

The Planning and Zoning Commission has on several occassions reviewed the Alexander request to construct a building on the above mentioned property and has denied the request because it was in violation of several sections of Ordinance No. 286 and against the wishes of the surrounding property owners. After our most recent denial on December 15, 1975, we were informed that although the Rules of Practice for the Planning and Zoning Commission had been adopted, and the record of that action can be found in the Planning and Zoning Commission minutes of January 17, 1972; the Rules of Practice were not then filed with the Secretary of State as required by the Wyoming Administrative Pro-ceedures Act. According to that act, "no agency, rule, order or decision is valid or effective against any person or property, or may it be invoked by the agency until it has been made available for public inspection as herein requir-ed." The "Public Inspection" referred to has been interpret-ed as being filed with the office of the Secretary of State. Due to the above mentioned act, our ruling regarding the Alexander request was declar-ed null and void.

Because of the legal techni-cality, the City Council was advised by the City Attorney that they should rule in favor of the construction of the Alexander Building.

The Planning and Zoning Commission strongly disap-proved of the action taken by the Council."

Uinta County Herald, October 28, 1976.

A special meeting was called by Mayor South with county commissioners and representatives from the Wyoming Highway Department. The meeting was called to discuss the problem of drainage coming off the Interstate Highway and the deteriorated condition of the underpass.

The highway department was in the process of replacing an old highway bridge over Bear River north of Evanston on Wyoming Highway 89. They were also improving the highway in some areas. City Engineer Proffit announced to the council that the highway department had agreed to give the old bridge that was removed from the highway to the City of Evanston. He said they would remove the old one-way bridge on Holland Drive and replace it with the bridge that they remove from Highway 89. He said they also agreed to widen Holland Drive and improve it. This would give Holland Drive a two-way bridge and drivers would no longer have to wait when another car had to cross the bridge. The new bridge would also handle heavier vehicles, making it more convenient for larger trucks.

At our next regular meeting James Phillips, City Attorney, presented the mayor with his letter of resignation effective immediately because he was going to run for County Attorney in the upcoming election. By accepting his resignation, we were without an attorney; therefore, Mayor South immediately asked Attorney Dennis Lancaster to fill in as the acting attorney until we could make it official. He accepted and later became officially the city attorney.

The November election was over and Jimmy Carter won the presidential election. In the city we had four new council members. Those elected were Russell "Bub" Albrecht for Ward 1, Jimmie Rice for Ward 2 and David Bills for Ward 3. Roy Fruits was elected to the two-year term that was left vacant by Rees "Tubb" Nichols. These four new council members would be joining holdovers Ron Davis and me.

Also, with just one four-year term open for election in the county commissioner's race, John Fanos won and would be joining holdovers William Megeath and Gene Martin. Gene Taylor from Mountain View did not seek re-election. Louise Karn was officially elected to the office of Justice of the Peace, a four-year term.

Gene Taylor and I were both still members of the Governor's Planning Committee on Criminal Administration when the report came out that there would be full funding available for constructing new facilities pertaining to law and criminology, such as courthouses and police facilities. I informed the mayor and council that we should be making application for new city facilities. They all agreed, so the mayor instructed me to draw up an application.

Gene Schrader, Grantsman, was hired by the city to make application for the grant, but applying through the Governor's Planning Committee funding could only be used for law enforcement facilities such as courthouses, police stations or county law enforcement buildings. So when Schrader made the application he had to describe the facility as a city courthouse and police station. He could not, by law, describe the building as a city hall, but that was okay with everyone and everyone was aware of the way the application was presented, because the building would be used for municipal court cases and the office of the city judge would be in the building. It would also house the Evanston Police Department, it would be used as the Evanston City Hall for city council meetings, and offices would be available for city personnel including the mayor. There was no doubt in anyone's mind that the city needed a new building. The old town hall had been built in 1911, and was almost 70 years old.

The next two meetings in November mainly consisted of the approval of more subdivisions. At this time most subdivisions were being developed by local land owners, but it wouldn't be much longer before we would have out-of-state builders and sub-dividers coming in to get a part of the action, especially if the oil and gas discovery got as big as it seemed to be getting. The housing problem was being well taken care of with all the new apartments and housing being built.

Also during the November meetings, the Parks and Recreation Commission presented the name of Dennis Poppinga as their choice for the position of Recreation Director for Evanston. After some discussion it was moved and then seconded that Poppinga be hired under contract for the first year. The motion passed with all voting in favor.

At our regular meeting in December, Mr. Dennis Poppinga was introduced to the council for the first time as the city's new recreation director. Mayor South and the council welcomed him and congratulated him on his new job. Poppinga stated that he was very excited about the position and said he knew he could do a good job and make the city proud.

Recreation Director Hired For Evanston

The City of Evanston has hired a recreation director, according to recreation commission chairman Ryley Dawson. The director, Dennis Poppinga will be in his programs in early December.

The Recreation Commission has been considering a variety of ideas for the improvement of the recreation program in Evanston. With the addition of a full-time director, it is hoped that many new programs can be added, as well as existing programs inproved. The commission is looking toward Poppinga as an "expert" who can implement the programs and increase activity.

Initially Poppinga is expected to handle many of the programs that operated under the jurisdiction of the community education program run by the school district last year. This included the operation of sports leagues at the various age levels. He will operate the ski program "He will work with existing programs and introduce new programs" according to Dawson.

Poppinga is now the district executive for a coed youth organization in the San Fernando Valley and West Los Angeles districts, according to

Dennis Popinga

Dawson. His job has been to organize youth groups and plan and direct activities such as campouts, olympics, and tournaments, Dawson says. He has also been the year round director for a 240 acre

camp.

Popinga is a former student at Bonneville High School in Ogden, Utah. He lettered three years each in football, basketball, baseball, and track. He was All Area in football, basketball and baseball. He lettered four years in football at Brigham Young University.

Popinga is married and has two children. His wife, Vickie, is a registered nurse.

He will be paid $12,000.00 annually, according to Dawson. While his salary has been in the city budget since July, it is expected that his work will gradually allow the city to phase out other areas of jurisdiction and combine them under the direction of the city parks and recreation director, thereby eliminating some current costs. Popinga will also be responsible for assisting in the acquiring of grants to assist with his salary and the running of the programs.

Uinta County Herald, November 18, 1976.

Dennis Poppinga was a graduate of Brigham Young University, where he played football on a scholarship and with academic honors. He ended up as the director of recreation and parks in Evanston for the next 39 years and raised a family of very athletic boys and girls. Dennis and his wife, a registered nurse, had both been real assets to the City of Evanston and had become good active citizens.

Mayor South also announced that Evanston's application for the city facility had been approved. He got word from not only our grants man, Mr. Schrader, but he also got a call from one of our U.S. Senators confirming that the grant had been approved by the U.S. Department of Commerce and the funding would be coming through the Governor's Planning Committee. The official letter stated that it would be a 100% grant and the city would have 90 days in which to begin ground-breaking. The site was already established at the corner of Main Street and 12th Street, where Time-DC Trucking was located.

Also during the meeting, Mayor South reported that he and I had met in Cheyenne with the U.S. Housing and Urban Development (HUD) group. He pointed out that there was a lot of money available for different projects and that Evanston should be looking into forming an Urban Renewal Agency soon, but it was a few years before that would happen.

The Wyoming Highway Department was also at the meeting to show the council some of the suggestions they had concerning a viaduct (overpass) over the railroad and river that would help take some of the load from the underpass.

There were several local business folks present at the meeting with many questions concerning how a new overpass, located elsewhere across the railroad tracks, would affect the businesses on Front Street and downtown area. Mayor South explained that he had no intentions of harming any business in Evanston, but with the present underpass being the only access to cross the tracks, other than going around the freeway (I-80), having a new viaduct would be extremely necessary, especially when the present underpass got overloaded with too much traffic or was flooded. Everyone seemed to agree, but they were all concerned where the location of the new overpass would be. That was an issue that would come up at a later date, provided by the Wyoming Highway Department. The City of Evanston did get the new viaduct but it was several more years before anything was completed.

There were some Evanston streets that needed to be improved because of the increase in traffic and additional subdivisions. After some discussion Councilman Lunsford made a motion authorizing City Attorney Dennis Lancaster to draw up a resolution of intent to create another Improvement District, seconded by me, all voting in favor.

1976 ended up being another very busy year, mostly because of the growing economy that was often causing changes in a lot of our ordinances, especially in the zoning, subdivisions and building, plus there was an influx of population driving the need for more housing. It was tough just trying to keep up.

CHAPTER 11

1977....The first regular meeting of 1977 started with the swearing in of the four new city council members, Albrecht, Rice, Bills and Fruits. They would be joining Davis and me as members of the council along with Mayor Dan South. The mayor had made no changes in his appointments, except to appoint Dennis Lancaster as Acting City Attorney after the resignation of James Phillips. During this meeting, Mr. Lancaster was officially appointed by the mayor and sworn in by Don Welling, City Clerk.

Mayor South called for a special meeting on January 12th to discuss a few resolutions. The first, introduced by Councilman Albrecht, was to authorize the mayor and the city clerk to enter into an agreement with the architectural firm Tom B. Muths and Associates to design the new city hall and law enforcement facility. The facility was to be financed by a grant received from the U.S. Department of Commerce, Economic Development Administration. Motion to adopt this resolution was made by Fruits, seconded by Rice, with all voting in favor.

Mayor South called for an introduction on the next resolution, which I provided. This resolution authorized the mayor and city clerk to enter into an agreement with Gene Schrader and Associates to act as project coordinator in construction of the city facility. A motion to adopt this resolution was made by Albrecht, seconded by Fruits, with all voting in favor.

The third and final resolution of the meeting was introduced by Councilman Rice. It authorized Mayor South and the city clerk to enter into an agreement with City Attorney Lancaster to act as the legal counsel for the city and its interest concerning the construction of the new facility. A motion to adopt the resolution was made by me, seconded by Bills, with all voting in favor.

After this meeting, it looked like we were finally going to get our new city facility, something the city had needed for years. It would be located on the corner of 12th and Main Street. Soil testing would be underway at the site by the end of January.

Mayor South called for another special meeting on January 20th to discuss the drilling of oil and gas wells within the city limits. The meeting was attended by a small group of interested citizens. A representative from Amoco, Mr. Ed Woodall, addressed the group and stated that all precautions would be taken to keep the operation safe. He said that he didn't expect any more than just the one well to be drilled within the limits of the city, but the next few years proved him wrong.

The Uinta County Herald issue dated January 27th came out with an article titled OIL WELL WILL BE DRILLED INSIDE THE CITY LIMITS. The article went on to say that Amoco would be drilling the well near what once were the U.P.R.R. gravel pits just west of the roundhouse. This article caused a lot of people to be concerned about safety because so much of the drilling in the area had been for gas as well as oil, and some of the gas was H2S, hydrogen sulfide, which is a sour gas and very poisonous. However, the oil companies assured everyone that every safety precaution would be taken to keep everyone safe.

By 1982 the City of Evanston had approximately twelve wells, oil and gas, drilled within the limits of the city. Some of them were included within city limits in the course of outward expansion during the boom period. Most of those within the city limits weren't as deep as the gas wells and were done by directional drilling for oil only. However, there were a few deep gas wells drilled inside or close by city limits that had some neighbors concerned.

On January 31, 1977, Mayor South called for a special meeting concerning an Improvement District. Notice was sent out to all property owners liable to assessment for the construction and installation of street paving, curb and gutters, drainage improvement, walks and storm sewers within proposed Special Improvement District No. 2. After a considerable amount of discussion, the majority of the property owners indicated that they were in favor of the Improvement District. Therefore, a resolution was introduced. A motion by the council was made and seconded, with all council members voting in favor. The city attorney and the city engineer were directed by the mayor to proceed with the paperwork and the bidding.

At the regular council meeting on February 2nd, Mr. Joe Evans, representing the Wyoming Department of Economic Planning and Development, and Commissioner Eugene B. Martin of the Uinta County Commission were present to request the city to adopt a resolution forming an association of government between the two neighboring counties (Uinta and Lincoln Counties). The resolution was already prepared and was introduced by me. It read that the City of Evanston had determined that it was in the best interest of the citizens of the city of Evanston to form a Joint Powers Board with the two counties. The resolution went on to state that the official name would be Lincoln Uinta Association of Governments (LUAG). The motion to adopt was passed with all voting in favor.

During the meeting, bids were opened for the purchase of a new police car, but with the shortage of funds in the police budget a motion was made and seconded that all bids be rejected. The motion was passed with all voting in favor.

Councilman Albrecht then made a motion that Police Chief Mel Wren be given permission to investigate the possibility of getting a used vehicle from the Wyoming Highway Patrol, seconded by Davis. The motion was passed with all voting in favor.

Other business that came up during the meeting was the request for a pay raise for those police officers who had just finished their training at the Police Academy in Douglas, Wyoming, but Mayor South was not in favor of giving any pay raises mid-year. Therefore the request was tabled until the time came to plan the budget for the next fiscal year.

Mr. Charles Albrecht presented the pre-application plans for the M–B Subdivision. Evanston's subdivision ordinance states that anyone subdividing must either dedicate to the city 5% of the land for public use, or pay 5% of the raw land value to the city. Mr. Marvin

Bollschweiler made a request that he be permitted to pay a percentage of the value of the land, subject to an appraisal, rather than contribute any land to the city for a public park.

But because there were no public parks or playgrounds in that area a motion was made by Bills, seconded by Fruits, that Mr. Bollschweiler's request be denied and he be required to dedicate land rather than pay the 5% of land value in his proposed subdivision. The motion was passed with all voting in favor.

A long discussion concerning the landfill came up. The new landfill would be between 40 and 60 acres of state property located on the northerly side of the East Service Road. Evanston would go into a long term lease with the state and the preparation of the landfill would start sometime in early spring of that year. The old city dumps would be cleaned up as soon as possible after the new landfill was ready for use.

The issue of the Federal Flood Insurance program came up and it was stated that for Evanston to be eligible to participate in the HUD program, the city needed to pass a resolution. Therefore, a resolution was introduced by Bills to allow the City of Evanston to determine flood plains or mudslide areas within limits of the city. A motion was made to adopt the resolution and was seconded. The motion was passed with all voting in favor.

That February, the Uinta County Herald had an article concerning the 55 mph speed limit of the interstate highways. The headline read, WYOMING DRIVERS IGNORE 55 MILES SPEED LIMIT. Apparently, the low speed limit was causing a lot of problems for the Wyoming Highway Patrol, because it was reported that about 76 percent of drivers exceeded the speed limit. This was causing the highway patrol to issue a lot of citations. The article stated that the patrol, in one month, wrote over 5,600 citations on Wyoming Interstates 80 and 25 and in the entire year of 1976 they wrote over 50,000. The truck drivers with their CB radios were causing a lot of problems, because they would tell other drivers the location of the highway patrol so they could slow down. The truck drivers' code name for patrol cars was "Magpies," because at that time patrol cars were black and white and easy to recognize.

The head of the Wyoming Highway Patrol made a statement at that time. He said, *It seems that a more logical conception for compliance might be to again try to sell the public on lower speeds by convincing them of the need, the savings and the reduction of fatalities and injuries.* Eventually they changed the speed limit to 75 mph. After all, the freeways were built for high speed, and the reasoning behind the lower speed limit was to save on gasoline because of the shortage, which turned out not to be all that serious.

During our regular council meeting on March 2nd, we acted on a few more ordinances and amended several of them. These ordinances pertained mostly to construction of new mains, regulations for construction, regulations governing the use of water and the water distribution system, and once again amending the animal control ordinance.

A news article in the Uinta County Herald early that spring stated that, according to a report from the U.S. Department of Agriculture, the Soil Conservation Service and the Wyoming State Engineer, the water outlook for our area was not encouraging. The article went on to say that potentially, summer water supplies for the lower Green and Bear River watersheds were poor. After reading this, the city knew that we would be rationing water another summer.

During the March meeting, there was a complaint concerning cleaning up the garbage in one of the new apartment complex areas. Apparently some of the tenants were not putting their garbage in the containers properly. It turned out that the complex did not have enough containers to take care of the number of tenants living in the apartments. More containers were provided by the city and the problem was taken care of.

Mr. Bollschweiler was present to present his preliminary plat of his M-B Subdivision. Mr. Proffit, City Engineer said he thought the plat met all specifications as far as design is concerned. Therefore Rice made a motion to approve the preliminary plat as presented, seconded by Bills. The motion passed with all voting in favor.

Mr. Bollschweiler asked us to reconsider the request that was denied at the February meeting where he proposed paying the city

5% of the raw land value rather than dedicating 5% of the property within the subdivision to the city for park use.

Since the last meeting of the Evanston Chamber of Commerce Mr. Bollschweiler apparently got some members to agree with him. So at the March meeting some of these people spoke up in favor of Bollschweiler's request. After discussion Mayor South asked for a motion to reconsider. Councilman Davis made a motion to reconsider the previous motion made at the last meeting, seconded by Rice. Mayor South called for a roll call vote on the motion. The results were as follows: Davis, Nay; Bills, Aye; Ottley, Nay; Fruits, Aye; Rice, Nay; Albrecht was absent. Motion to deny the request failed with the majority voting Nay.

With the motion denied, the City of Evanston ended up having the 5% land of the subdivision dedicated to the city for a park, but it was years before the city would have funds to landscape and complete the improvements to the park.

Today that property is Railroad Park, near the North Elementary School. Besides the playground equipment there is a U.P.R.R. box car and the old switch engine. That is why the park was named Evanston's Railroad Park. The old switch engine was given to the county and city after they shut the reclamation plant down. It was a small steam locomotive that was used to switch railroad cars around the yard. It is the same engine that was located on the Uinta County Courthouse yard in the location where the old gazebo was. The county commissioners were glad to get rid of the old engine, but it had been sitting in the courtyard for 12 years before it was moved to Railroad Park.

When Evanston was really booming in the 1980s the county decided to give the engine to the city for the park. At that time the county was enlarging the courthouse and needed the yard space for expansion. They moved the old engine to its present location at Railroad Park in 1982.

There was no way the city or county could move it with their equipment, so Brown and Root, Inc., a local company affiliated

with the oil industry, hired at their own expense Bunning Trucking out of Rock Springs to move it with one of their heavy trucks.
The only route available to move the engine from the courthouse
yard to the park area at that time was by going around to the west
exit of the freeway to the east exit of the freeway to get to the park.
The engine was too high for the underpass and too high and wide
to get across the tracks near the depot because of overhead power
lines and other obstructions. Neither the overpass off 6th Street nor
the Wyoming State Highway 150 freeway exit had been constructed at that time.

Mayor South called for a special meeting on March 29th to open
bids for the new city hall and law enforcement facility. The architect,
Thomas Muths and Associates, had called for electrical and mechanical bids to be opened first and they would be incorporated into the
General Contractor's bid, which would be opened later.

Following a recess to give the council an opportunity to review
the bids, motion was made by me to accept the low bid of $53,650
from Delcon, Inc. from Jackson, Wyoming for electrical and the
low bid of $204,739 from Berger Plumbing, also from Jackson, for
mechanical. The motion was seconded by Councilman Davis. The
mayor asked for a roll call vote with Albrecht voting aye; Fruits, aye;
Rice, aye; me, aye; Bills, aye; Davis, aye. For some reason Mayor
South decided to vote on the bid and voted nay, I don't recall why,
and he called for a recess to give the General Contractor time to
assemble their bids.

After the General Contractor bids were opened and a short discussion was held, Mayor South asked for a motion to adjourn to go
into executive session. Motion was made by Fruits, seconded by Rice,
with all voting in favor.

At 10:00 p.m. the Council was called back to order with Councilman Rice making the motion to accept the base bid of Darrell
W. Anderson Construction, Inc., from Logan, Utah, in the amount
of $655,000, seconded by Fruits with all voting in favor.

A resolution was executed for the purpose of authorizing the mayor and city clerk to enter into an agreement with Anderson Construction, as General Contractors, for the construction of the city hall and law enforcement facility. At that time the contracts had not been awarded pending the study of the low bids and a report from City Attorney Dennis Lancaster.

After several warnings by the Department of Environmental Quality (D.E.Q.) concerning the burning at the old city dumps, and a lawsuit filed against the City of Evanston by D.E.Q., the city announced that we had a location and that the new landfill would be ready for public use in April. That made D.E.Q. very happy and they immediately dropped the lawsuit. The new landfill would be located at the far eastern end of the East Service Road.

At this time the Evanston Police Department was manned by only nine police officers, including the chief, a full time secretary, who also doubled as a meter maid, a part time animal control officer and ten active voluntary reserve officers. One of the reserves was a female who also assisted with some of the secretarial work. The E.P.D. only had four police vehicles. The Uinta County Herald was quite concerned with how they were handling the city's police problems because of the fast growth. The city was growing in population at a relatively fast pace and was expanding into the county more and more each month through the development of new subdivisions and annexations.

A representative of the Herald decided to do a study of the E.P.D. to determine how well the city's under-manned department was handling the problems. The newspaper representatives talked to members of the department, they talked to the mayor and some of the council members, and they surveyed some of the business owners and other citizens.

The full time officers on the force were Chief Mel Wren, Assistant Chief Dennis Harvey, Sgt. Frank Chisholm, Sgt. Dean Forman, and officers, Larry Hendrix, Bruce Waters, Forrest Bright, Bob Prior and Dennis Layton. Paul Mitchell was the animal control officer and Jerry Liechty was the secretary.

Mayor South and the city council members were all of the opinion that the department was doing a good job, although the study did show that Evanston had fewer policemen for its population than the national average. After the study was completed the Uinta County Herald published in their newspaper an article titled QUIETLY AND EFFICIENTLY DOING THEIR JOB.

On March 23rd, the U.S. Department of Housing and Urban Development (HUD) announced that the City of Evanston and Uinta County had been accepted into the National Flood Insurance Program. This made a lot of the home owners happy, especially those who lived in the North Evanston area where the Bear River runs through.

At the April 6th meeting a Mr. Dan Nicholls approached the city council concerning the new landfill. He was interested in contracting with the city to maintain the landfill, but it was decided that the city would maintain it with city employees.

Also, City Engineer Proffit presented plans for Improvement District No. 2 and a schedule of events for the Improvement District and specifications. After a brief discussion, a resolution approving plans, specifications and the estimated cost was introduced by Councilman Fruits. A motion was made by me to adopt the resolution, seconded by Bills. The motion passed with all voting in favor.

Proffit also presented a plat and specifications for a special water project. After a short discussion, Councilman Albrecht made the motion that a call for bids be advertised for the project, seconded by Rice, with all voting in favor.

General Foreman Allen Kennedy announced that the new landfill would be ready for operation on April 18th, and he requested permission to hire two more employees, which would be needed. Permission was granted.

In other business, we approved several liquor licenses, and passed Ordinance No. 325 on third and final reading. This ordinance pertained to administrative procedures in the appointment of officers, duties of appointed officers, and repealing all previous ordinances pertaining to same. The approval of Ordinance No. 325 was passed with all voting in favor.

A discussion came up concerning an increase in the pay of the mayor and city council. At present, the mayor was receiving $100.00 per month and the members of the city council were getting $10.00 per meeting attended. There were no additional benefits provided to the mayor or council. We also discussed additional benefits for the employees such as health and retirement, but all the discussion ended with no other action taken at this time.

We also adopted Ordinance No. 326 on third and final reading. This ordinance concerned the rules and restrictions pertaining to animal control. Motion was made by Bills, seconded by Fruits, with all voting in favor.

Ordinance No. 329, pertaining to water distribution and to set the consumer's fees for use of water, came up for second reading. Motion was made by Albrecht to approve the ordinance on second reading, seconded by Fruits, with all voting in favor.

Mayor South called for a special meeting on April 21st to discuss and to act on Ordinance No. 329 on the third and final reading. There was a lot of controversy from the public concerning the ordinance, so the mayor had the city clerk post notices of the meeting in the local paper and send out notices with the billings to let everyone know that any concerned citizen should attend the meeting.

This brought quite a large crowd of interested citizens to the meeting. Most citizens were concerned over the new water rates. After the ordinance was read in full and a long period of discussion was held, City Attorney Lancaster recommended that the mayor and city council go into an executive session prior to passing the ordinance on the third and final reading. He indicated that there were certain items in the ordinance that should probably be discussed. The motion to go into executive session was made by Albrecht, seconded by me, with all voting in favor. The mayor and council then left the room and went into executive session in the small meeting room.

After coming out of a short session Mayor South called the meeting back to order. During the session there was discussion on certain items, but there were no changes or amendments recommended.

Therefore, Fruits made the motion to pass Ordinance No. 329 on third and final reading, seconded by Rice, with all voting in favor.

Councilman Fruits then introduced Ordinance No. 330, an ordinance that pertained to the disposal of garbage, solid waste and refuse, setting fees for the collection and the use of the new landfill. After the reading of the ordinance a motion was made by Fruits to pass on the first reading, seconded by Albrecht with all voting in favor.

Councilman Bills talked about his discussion with the Wyoming Highway Department concerning traffic lights in the city. Mayor South and the council instructed Councilman Bills to mention traffic lights at 11th and Main Street, and 9th and Front Street. The mayor and council felt that these locations were most important at this time.

Friday, April 15th Amoco Production Company announced that they would be shutting down one of their oil wells within the city limits because it had not shown the possibility of any production. The well was located in the northeast part of the city, near the cemetery.

County Attorney James Phillips had received the final official results recently completed in Uinta County by the U.S. Census Bureau. The census showed a total population in the county of 9,974 with Evanston having 4,829, which was 400 more than the last census. Lyman had a census count of 2,002 and Mountain View had 597.

Although the city of Evanston, among the other towns in Uinta County, was not satisfied with the census, they did accept the report. An accurate report was very important to the county and communities, because most revenues received were based on the population count; revenues such as sales tax and all other taxes the state collects off of all minerals, including oil and gas.

On April 1, 1977 Mayor South broke ground with the first shovelful of dirt at the groundbreaking ceremony for the new Evanston City Hall. The contract for the new structure had been awarded to Darrell Anderson of Logan, Utah. Completion would take approximately 18 months. Those present at the ceremony were Mayor South; City Council members Albrecht, Davis and me; City Clerk Don Welling and his assistant Phyllis Martin, General Foreman Allen Kennedy and Chief of Police Mel Wren.

At the regular city council meeting on May 4th we passed Ordinance No. 330 on second reading. This ordinance concerned the disposal of garbage, solid waste and refuse, and set fees for the collection of garbage and use of the new landfill. Motion was made by me and seconded by Albrecht. The motion passed with all voting in favor.

Also, Mayor South presented a letter of resignation from Police Chief Mel Wren to be effective June 1, 1977. He stated that he was resigning for personal reasons, indicating that he would be leaving Evanston. The mayor and city council, after a short discussion, accepted Wren's letter and wished him well in his new ventures. A short discussion followed on who would be worthy of the position, but no other action was taken at that time.

THURSDAY, APRIL 7, 1977

Page eleven UINTA COUNTY HERALD Evanston, Wyoming

Groundbreaking For New City Hall

Evanston Mayor Dan L. South, left, lifts the first shovelful of dirt at groundbreaking ceremonies for the new Evanston City Hall Friday morning, April 1st, 1977. The contract for the new structure has been awarded to Darrell Anderson of Logan, Utah for the total amount of $695,300.00. He will be responsible for sub-contracting electrical and mechanical work on the project. According to the contract Mr. Anderson has 18 months to complete the construction, which would be December of 1978. He says, however, that it should be completed well ahead of that time. Others in the photo above, besides Mayor South, are: left to right, Mr. South, City Councilmen Russell Albrecht and Ronald Davis, Deputy City Clerk Phyllis Martin, City Clerk Don U. Welling, Shop Foreman Allen Kennedy, Councilman Dennis Ottley, and Police Chief Mel Wren.

Due to the water shortage this year, Councilman Fruits made a motion that beginning May 15th water use be rationed by using the odd and even house number system. The motion was seconded by Councilman Bills, all voting in favor.

Also that month Mr. Albert Pilch of the Wyoming Recreation Commission presented a check in the amount of $18,469.73 to be used to help build the new tennis courts. Mayor South stated that the construction of the two new courts would be a much needed addition to the city's recreation program, and thanked Mr. Pilch for all his assistance in obtaining these funds for the city.

Mayor South called for a special meeting to be held on May 31st at the Uinta County Court House because the meeting called for the discussion of Ordinance No. 333, pertaining to the confirmation of Special Improvement District No. 2. The ordinance was expected to be passed on first reading as an emergency, and the mayor expected a large attendance of citizens that the ordinance would affect.

The meeting did turn out to have a large attendance, too many for the small council room at the city hall building. During the meeting, there didn't seem to be much opposition, because most of the folks involved were property owners that would be in favor of the improvements.

Ordinance No. 333 was introduced by Councilman Albrecht. After the ordinance was read by the attorney a motion was made by me to suspend the rules and allow the ordinance to be passed by emergency, seconded by Rice. The motion passed with all voting in favor.

Next, a motion was made by me to pass the ordinance on the first reading as an emergency, seconded by Albrecht, with all voting in favor. Therefore, Mayor South declared the ordinance to be duly adopted and recorded as required by law.

During our regular meeting of June 8th, Mr. Earl O'Driscoll from the United States Forest Service was present and made a request to the council to allow the forest service the use of the new landfill site for refuse from forest campsites. A short discussion followed with the council agreeing to the request, but the landfill use fee would be set at $8.00 per load plus a $200.00 surcharge. Mr. O'Driscoll agreed to the conditions and Councilman Albrecht introduced a resolution establishing the agreement. Motion was made by Rice and seconded by Fruits. The resolution passed with all voting in favor.

During the meeting Mayor South assigned Dennis Harvey as Acting Chief of Police, since Chief Mel Wren had submitted his resignation. Harvey would oversee the duties of the chief until a permanent appointment was made.

Acting Chief Harvey made his report, which included some problems and complaints concerning the vandalism and late night parties that were being held at Hamblin Park. He requested that the park be shut down during the late hours.

After some discussion Councilman Fruits made a motion to close the park between the hours of 11:00 p.m. and 7:00 a.m., seconded by Bills. Motion passed with all voting in favor. Attorney Lancaster informed us that an ordinance would have to be prepared pertaining to the hours set for use of the park. Mayor South directed Lancaster to prepare the ordinance and have it ready for the next meeting.

Since the new census had been taken of the population of the City of Evanston there had been a terrific loss of revenue to the city. The loss had been estimated as much as $200,000 by this time. Therefore, it was the decision of the mayor and council to contest the most recent census. The Uinta County Herald issue of May 26th read, CITY TO OFFICIALLY CONTEST CENSUS. It said that the mayor and council had further reservations about the accuracy of the census when reports began to be received of families that were not contacted during the census. Over 200 people had reported that they were never counted, and the mayor estimated that there were probably others that had not been counted as well.

Mayor South contacted the Census Bureau concerning the situation, but the bureau stated that the City of Evanston would have to present proof that these people had not been counted. They stated that according to the bureau's records the folks that reported they had not been contacted had actually been counted, and that the city would have to show additional proof before they would do another census.

The city made an effort to contact all residences within the city asking them the following question: *If you were not counted during the last census, and live within the city limits, please contact City Clerk Don Welling at the City Hall and give him your name.*

A special meeting was called by the mayor on June 15th to start at 5:00 p.m., mainly to have the Budget Officer present the tentative budget to the City Council, but there was other business to act on as well.

Ordinance No. 334 came up for a second reading. This was an ordinance to adopt and enact a new code of ordinances. It was moved by me, seconded by Fruits, to pass on second reading with all voting in favor.

Ordinance No. 335 was introduced by Councilman Albrecht. This ordinance was to establish the hours for use of Hamblin Park. The hours set for use of the park would be from 7:00 a.m. to 11:00 p.m. Because of the problems the city was having during late hours at the park, it was suggested that this ordinance be passed on first reading as an emergency. A motion to suspend the rules was made by Councilman Davis, seconded by Fruits, with all voting in favor.

A motion to adopt on emergency basis and pass into law on first reading was made by Fruits and seconded by me. The motion passed with all voting in favor.

The proposed budget presented by the Budget Officer then came up for consideration. There were a lot of questions from the council concerning the budget as proposed, but after a long and lengthy discussion a motion to accept the proposed budget was made by me and seconded by Fruits. The motion passed with all voting in favor.

A discussion took place concerning job descriptions for the employees. Allen Kennedy was officially named General Superintendent of Public Works. Raymond Gerrard and James Bateman would be Water Plant Engineers, Eugene Slagowski would be Cemetery Sexton, Fay Riebennacht would oversee the wastewater (sewer) plant. Jack Day would oversee the water department, James Bruce would oversee the street department and Verdon Moore would oversee the solid waste (garbage) department. Dennis Poppinga would continue to oversee Parks and Recreation. Thomas (Butch) Whittaker, Ross

Easton and Wayne Kautz were named as lead workers, while all other employees would be known as operators.

Finally, with no other business, the meeting adjourned by motion at 12:35 a.m. of June 16th.

Animal control has always been a big problem for the City of Evanston, but in the past we never had the funds to hire a full-time animal control officer or lease a decent location to house stray pets. However, we finally got the state to allow the city to use part of the old armory, due to the finishing of the new armory.

We set up a very poor ventilated section in the old armory for use as an animal control pound. We improved the area to meet the standards for a halfway decent place for stray animals. Rhonda Teachenor was acting as part-time animal control officer at the time, but with the new fiscal year coming up she had been budgeted for full time. With this change the city was able to control the animal problem much better, but the mayor said that; *we still needed to look for a new location to build a new pound sometime in the near future, maybe in the vicinity of the new landfill,* he suggested. We knew that the state would be tearing down the old armory sometime in the near future.

Our regular meeting of July 6th was another long and drawn out meeting consisting mostly of unfinished business. There were requests for water hookups outside the city limits by various folks who lived out of town. Mayor South directed the City Engineer John Proffit to study the situation and City Attorney Lancaster to look into the legalities of selling water outside the city limits.

Mr. Jim Anderson of Hannifer, Imhoff and Sanford, Inc. of Denver, Colorado requested the opportunity to sell the bonds for Improvement District No. 2. He explained his offer and reasons to go with his company. The proposition he presented sounded good.

Therefore, after a lengthy discussion, Councilman Fruits made a motion for the city to enter into an agreement with Hannifer, Imhoff and Sanford to sell the Improvement District No. 2 bonds, seconded by me. The motion passed with all voting in favor.

Ordinance No. 336 was then introduced by Fruits, an ordinance authorizing the issuance of the Special Improvement District No. 2

bonds. It was then moved by Fruits and seconded by Bills to suspend the rules and pass this ordinance on an emergency basis, with all voting in favor, including the mayor. Councilman Fruits then made a motion to pass Ordinance No. 336, seconded by Davis, with all voting in favor.

Ordinance No. 337 was then introduced by me. This was an ordinance setting forth the interest rate on installments of assessment for Special Improvement District No. 2. After being read in full and with some discussion, Councilman Rice made the motion to suspend the rules and pass Ordinance No. 337 on an emergency basis, seconded by me. All voted in favor.

A motion followed by Bills to pass Ordinance No. 337 on an emergency basis, seconded by Fruits, with all voting in favor.

A resolution was passed by the city council setting the fee for dumping at the Evanston Landfill by the Wyoming State Highway Department. All members of the council voted in favor.

Ordinance No. 334 also came up for third and final reading. This was an ordinance to adopt and enact into law a new code of ordinances for the City of Evanston. It was moved and seconded with all voting in favor.

Also, a resolution was introduced by me to set days and time for hours of operation for the new city landfill. It was moved and seconded and all voted in favor.

City Attorney Lancaster asked for permission to start to re-codify the ordinances. He stated this was something that should have been done years ago, but hadn't, and Evanston needed to get this project started immediately, because it was going to take a lot of time, and it did. We didn't get this project completed until a couple years later.

President Jimmy Carter designated an emergency in Uinta and Sublette Counties in Wyoming and made the counties eligible for emergency loans because of damages and losses caused by the drought. This was effective on June 17th with an application deadline of August 18th of that same year. I don't remember Evanston asking for any assistance, but I'm sure the counties did.

This was probably one of the worst years for drought Evanston and Uinta County had ever had. It was so bad that we didn't just go with the odd and even house number system, but we also limited watering to certain hours. If I remember right, watering was only permitted between the hours of 6:00 p.m. to 9:00 a.m.

This was also a period when all the cafes and restaurants went to rationing water. To get a glass of water with your order you had to ask for it. The restaurants were no longer furnishing water to your table without you requesting it. That was how bad the shortage of water was during this drought period. Most restaurants were good about it giving you water when you requested it, but they were very concerned about the drought and how long it would last. If I remember right it only lasted the one year. Next year, hopefully, would be better.

The new Uinta County Criminal Justice Building (the Uinta County jail facility) was dedicated and opened on June 15th. Funding for the facility was provided by the Wyoming State Planning Committee on Criminal Administration, which Commissioner Gene Taylor and I were members of at the time.

In the June 30th issue of the Uinta County Herald was an article concerning a local gambling arrest, titled OFFICIALS DISQUALIFIED IN LOCAL GAMBLING CASE. Apparently there was a friendly poker game going on at the establishment of a local business. At that time gambling was illegal in the State of Wyoming, even poker. An officer of the Evanston Police Department and Deputy of the Uinta County Sheriff's Office were the arresting officers. Obviously they were aware of the game going on and decided to make a raid on the group. The game was going on upstairs in the building. There were several upstanding and well respected Evanston citizens involved. Arrests were made and the criminal complaints, made by the city officer, read, *the group was unlawfully playing poker with cards for money and poker chips constituting the representative of value by playing the same in an upper room of the building.*

Also, an additional second complaint was filed by the city officer against the owners of the building. They were also charged for *allowing the game to be played in their building.*

At that time, Justice of the Peace was Louise Karn and the County Attorney was James Phillips. Both disqualified themselves from participating in any proceedings connected with the alleged gambling incident in the early hours of June 22nd. Both cited a conflict of interest as the reason for dismissing themselves. Mr. Phillips stated that he had business interests with some of the accused men, and Mrs. Karn stated that one of the accused was a relative through marriage. Therefore, District Judge C. Stuart Brown had to appoint new officers to handle the case and would announce a date for arraignment later on.

In spite of the city ordinance prohibiting fireworks within the city limits, there was a haze and the smell of fireworks in the air on the 4th of July that year, and fireworks were on every street. The Uinta County Herald issue of July 7th had an article labeled CITY FULL OF FIREWORKS ON 4th OF JULY WEEKEND. The article went on to say that Kilburn Porter, owner and operator of a fireworks stand outside of town, said that the reason fireworks were so popular was probably because of the nation's bicentennial in 1976. He said, *Last year was the biggest the fireworks industry ever had.*

Porter was asked about rumors that the authorities had closed his stand to prevent the purchase of fireworks near the city in a year of drought, but the truth was that he shut down the stand earlier this particular year; *for reasons of health,* he said. *Our help was tired out from overworking,* he added.

He noted that fireworks had been a big tourist attraction in Wyoming for some time. Surprisingly, he stated that he favors more state regulations. He said, *I think we should be set up as a state dealer, similar to the way the liquor industry is.*

Fireworks, at that time, were legal in the state and county, but most cities and towns made them illegal within the town or city limits of those communities. Evanston had an ordinance against fireworks, except for the 4th of July display that one of the local organizations put on every year by permit. This particular year no club or organization put one on because it was so dry, so the public went a little wild on the fireworks, but no damage was done except there were remains of used fireworks on about every street in town that had to be cleaned up by the city crew, and we had complaints about the smell. It seemed like we had a few complaints every year because of fireworks after the 4th, though a lot of the folks actually appreciated them, but only during the holiday.

On August 3rd the City of Evanston held its regular meeting. After the motion to accept the minutes and pay the bills, Mayor South appointed Dennis Harvey as Evanston's Chief of Police. I made the motion to confirm the appointment, seconded by Albrecht. The motion passed with all voting in favor. Councilman Albrecht then made the motion to appoint Officer Frank Chisholm as Assistant Chief, seconded by Davis, with all voting in favor.

After the adoption of Ordinance No. 334, an ordinance to adopt and enact a new code of ordinances, City Attorney Lancaster suggested we change the numbering of future ordinances such that the first ordinance would be numbered 77-1, indicating the year and the number of the ordinance. This would be the time to do this, while we are in the process of re-codifying the ordinances, he said. Mayor South and the council agreed to his decision with no objections.

Chief Harvey announced that since the new Public Safety Building had been finished all city arrests that were taken to jail would be taken to the new county facility. He stated that he had a tentative budget to present to the city for proposed expenses to Uinta County for the use of their Public Safety Building. He also gave his monthly report to the council.

Ordinance 77-1 was introduced by Councilman Bills. This ordinance was to amend and re-enact Section 2-4 of the revised code of the City of Evanston, Wyoming, 1977, providing for the salaries of the mayor and council members.

The ordinance went on to say that the annual salaries of the following officers of the city for the respective positions held by them would be paid in twelve monthly installments as follows: Mayor, $7,200.00 annually ($600.00 monthly), and Council Members, $1,800.00 annually ($150.00 monthly). This was an increase for the mayor from $100.00 per month to $600.00 per month, and an increase to the council members from $10.00 per meeting to $150.00 per month.

A motion to pass this ordinance on first reading was made by me, seconded by Albrecht, with all voting in favor.

Councilman Bills followed by introducing Ordinance 77-2. This was an ordinance to amend and re-enact Section 19-16 (D) (2) (1) of the code providing for an owner of land to be subdivided to convey part of the proposed subdivision to the city for parks and recreation purposes, or at the option of the city, in lieu of such conveyance of land, pay to the city a cash amount of the raw land value.

Motion to pass on first reading was made by Bills, seconded by me, all voting in favor.

The action on all these new numbered ordinances was the start of the project to re-codify the city's ordinances and get shed of some of the old outdated laws that had been on the books so long and were no longer in use. This would be a long, drawn out project that would probably take at least two years to complete.

That same meeting Ordinance 77-3 was also introduced by Councilman Bills. This was an ordinance to amend and re-enact the code to provide for the creation of the Evanston Planning and Zoning Commission, duties of the commission, terms of the commissioners and staff, and providing for the replacement of commission members and filling vacancies.

A motion to pass on first reading was made by me, seconded by Davis, all voting in favor.

Representatives from the Liquor Dealers Association were in attendance at the meeting to meet with the council. They had previously asked for all liquor license applications to expire on the same day each year. The attorney had explained to them that this would have to be done by ordinance. The group had asked that the date for license renewal be on October 15th of each year.

Ordinance 77-5, pertaining to the liquor licenses, had been prepared and was ready to be acted upon at this meeting. Ordinance 77-5 was an ordinance to amend the revised code of the City of Evanston and providing for a uniform expiration date for liquor licenses of October 15 of each year, providing for the pro-ration of existing licenses to October 15, 1978. The ordinance was introduced by Councilman Bills. After Attorney Lancaster read the ordinance, a lengthy discussion took place concerning the prices on liquor licenses and other issues. Mayor South said that we would discuss these issues at a later time, but right now we need a motion to act on the ordinance presently on the floor. Motion was made by Bills to pass Ordinance 77-5 on first reading as amended, seconded by me. The motion passed with all voting in favor.

On August 4th the Uinta County Herald reported that AMOCO GAUGES OVERTHRUST BELT DISCOVERY AT 4.7 MILLION CUBIC FEET. This looked like the oil and gas industry was getting bigger than expected and Evanston was looking at a large impact of people.

The local newspaper also announced in the same issue that Pat Swauger was appointed Treasurer of Uinta County on Tuesday, August 2nd. District Judge C. Stuart Brown administered the oath of office

The first seven months of this year appeared to be another very busy year and Mayor South seemed to be doing a good job handling things, but then on Sunday, August 7th one of Evanston's worst tragedies happened.

About 3:30 a.m. early that Sunday three members of an Evanston family were killed: Attorney Vincent A. Vehar, age 67; his wife Beverly Mudd Vehar, age 52; and their son John Vehar, age 18. The tragedy was caused when their brick home was demolished by an explosion with immense intensity.

A fourth family member, an older son, Anthony V. (Tony) Vehar, age 27, was seriously injured, but miraculously escaped death. He was taken to the Uinta County Memorial Hospital and was later reported to be in fair condition.

The blast was of such force that it was heard and felt in most areas of town. As far as five or six blocks away windows rattled and houses vibrated. The home next door had to be completely replaced because the blast caused extreme damage to the foundation.

The Vehar home was completely leveled and reduced to nothing but a pile of rubble. It was one of the most horrendous criminal acts that had ever happened in Uinta County. The family was a very well respected and prominent family in the county. Mr. Vehar had been County Attorney and more recently had been Evanston's city attorney for several years.

The Vehar family, including Mr. and Mrs. Vehar, and their sons Tony and John had been in Laramie, Wyoming. They had gone on Friday to attend the Fourth Annual Shrine All-Star Football Game, which was played Saturday afternoon. John was a player on the South All-Star team in the game, and had the possibility of receiving a football scholarship from the University of Wyoming. Tony, who was a practicing attorney in Kemmerer, Wyoming had come to Evanston to accompany the family to Laramie.

Their only daughter, Kathy Vehar Holgate, and her small daughter had remained in Evanston. She resided in her own apartment, and was not at the family home.

Although some neighbors had not expected the Vehars to return home until Sunday, they returned late Saturday or very early Sunday morning. One neighbor reported seeing lights on in the Vehar home about 1:30 a.m.

Police officers were summoned to the site about 3:40 a.m. by neighbors, who reported the explosion. The officers then alerted the Fire Department who sounded a general alarm. About thirty volunteer firemen responded and were on the scene within minutes.

At first they thought that the explosion may have been set off by a natural gas leak, but after calling in state and federal officials to help with the investigation they finally determined it was an intentional bombing. Sheriff Leonard Wilson reported days later that a laboratory report from the U.S. Treasury Department's Bureau of Alcohol, Tobacco and Firearms had positively identified dynamite in the bomb that demolished the Vehar home.

Evidence gathered from the scene of the predawn explosion had been sent to the laboratory shortly after the incident, and the sheriff had been waiting for the report ever since. He said the report contained no further information.

We lived about 6 or 7 blocks from the scene of the blast but didn't hear or feel a thing. My wife, my youngest son Cody and I were scheduled to leave Evanston early that same morning to go to Crawford, Nebraska to attend our son, David's wedding. So we never heard much about the incident until we got back home, and what we heard was very disturbing. We couldn't believe such a horrifying act could happen in Evanston.

When I got back to town and heard some of the details of what happened, I immediately got hold of Mayor South to discuss the incident with him. He told me that as soon as it was reported by the police officers first on the scene they immediately called him. He immediately got dressed and went to the scene. He told me that as soon as he saw the house blown to bits and nothing but a pile of rubble it really got to him. He said as he walked through the debris he noticed a body lying in the rubble and, with tears in his eyes, he said it was Mrs. Vehar and that she just looked like a little rag doll laying there. As he told me of the findings that early Sunday morning he had me almost in tears also. He said it was the most devastating thing he had ever seen.

Apparently the whole thing was caused by a dispute between a property owner in Fort Bridger, Mark Hopkinson, who owned a mobile home park, and the Bridger Valley Sewer District in which Vince Vehar was acting as their legal counsel. For some reason or other, the owner of the property had really gotten upset about some problem that he had with Vehar.

I am not going to go into any details of the investigation or the court proceedings in this book, because there has been so much written about it, and besides, the case got so complicated over the months with other deadly criminal acts that turned out to be related to the case. The entire case was eventually given to the already-famous Jerry Spence law office. After months and months of investigating and court hearings, the case was finally solved and the responsible party, Mark Hopkinson, was found guilty and received the death penalty. He was sent to the Wyoming State Penitentiary where he was eventually executed.

During the investigation Mayor South called for a meeting with County Attorney James Phillips and Sheriff Leonard Wilson and city council members. There was a rumor that Sheriff Wilson had got wind that Mark Hopkinson had put out notice that he would be hiring a hit man to do away with all elective officials in Uinta County. I asked Wilson how serious this was and how long he had known about the threat. He indicated that it was nothing to take lightly, knowing Hopkinson like he does, and that he had known about the threat for quite some time. Well, I got a little upset because he had kept it quiet for so long, and told him that if someone was threatening me or my family that I wanted to know about it immediately so I could do something about it. He said that he didn't blame me for being upset, and apologized to everyone in attendance for not letting us know sooner. We all took the threat pretty seriously, especially the county attorney and sheriff, because they were right in the middle of the investigation. All elected officials in the county were very concerned and took whatever precautions were necessary to protect their family.

I took extra precautions to protect my family by taking Cody, my youngest son, to school and picking him up after school every day for a while. At that time Cody was the only one of our four sons still at home. My other three sons were all away from home and married, and had their own families to worry about, but they were well aware of the threat. Sometimes, especially on weekends, I would take my wife Sandy and Cody and go to Green River, Wyoming and visit my oldest son and his family and stay for a few days.

A threat from Hopkinson was nothing to take lightly, because not too long after we heard about the threats, he was sentenced to serve time in a federal prison somewhere in California. If I remember right, he was convicted on a drug distribution charge in Arizona and sent to prison, but while he was in the federal prison, the Vehar investigation was still going on. While there he had access to a telephone and hired a couple of hit men out of Utah to not only kill one of his henchmen that allegedly took part in the bombing, but to torture him first.

Hopkinson's friend that the hit was on was Jeff Green from Bridger Valley. When the hired hit men caught Green, it was said that they tortured the hell out of him first before killing him. Apparently, the word was out that Green was going to talk to the authorities on what had happened.

Having Hopkinson in prison took a lot of worry off the elected officials, so we all kind of settled down and went back to our regular life, but when the Green assassination took place it proved to us that even in prison Hopkinson could be dangerous. But the investigation was going right along and when the case was given to the Spence Law Firm, it wasn't too long before he was sentenced to prison in Rawlins and eventually was put to death.

This crime is on record and there have been plenty of information and books written about it. If anyone wants to find out more about the Vehar bombing, they can get it through almost any source, but because this happened during Mayor South's administration I had to mention it in this story.

The oil and gas discovery in the Overthrust Belt, Northeast Utah and Evanston area were becoming the center of a lot of attention at this time. There were getting to be a large number of drilling rigs coming into the area. A report from the oil industry announced that the activity remained very strong.

The Uinta County Assessor reported that there would be a large increase in tax revenue this fiscal year which would be helping the county, cities and towns, largely because of the oil and gas activity and the increase of industries and businesses that had moved into town. The Uinta County Herald in one of their latest issues had an article titled IMPACT CONTINUES IN COUNTY. The article said the development of coal, oil and gas will be the vehicle which will produce the impact.

The article went on to say that Rocky Mountain Energy, the Union Pacific company developing coal and other mining sources, is currently projecting their South Haystack Coal Mine would be in operation in 1978. It would employ approximately 300 employees, and their families would need a place to live.

Hearing the news that the Haystack mine was going to open up was great, but it didn't happen. At the time we never heard too much of why it didn't get going, but it was talked about a lot and there was no reason not to believe it would become a reality. The citizens of Uinta County were really looking forward to it, especially after the oil and gas boom became a bust. However, to this date the mine has still not been put into operation. The public seems to blame the U.S. Environmental Protection Agency (E.P.A.) for stopping it.

During the regular meeting of September 7th, after the initial business was taken care of, there was a long discussion concerning the incident at the Vehar home. Everyone seemed to be very concerned and expressed their sorrow for the Vehar family. Someone indicated that the family would be very much missed and how much the family had contributed to the City of Evanston. It was our first meeting since the incident and everyone seemed to be a bit depressed, especially while the subject was being discussed. During his monthly report to the council, Chief Harvey mentioned the Vehar bombing, but didn't have much information on it yet, but he said the bombing was under investigation and that state and federal officials were working with the sheriff's department in finding clues and details of what happened and why.

Also during the meeting, Fire Chief Jerry Cazin reported that there had been some promotions made in the department since Captain Royce Bills had resigned and moved to Salt Lake City, Utah. He stated that Benny Goodman would remain as Assistant Chief, Jon Lunsford would replace Bills as Captain, Jim Potter and Lee Bodine would both be promoted to Lieutenant, and Lynn Richards would continue to be Secretary-Treasurer.

Other business that came up was calling for bids on many pieces of old equipment that should have been replaced years ago, but now with the increase in tax revenues the city was in a position to replace some of that older equipment.

Ordinances 77-1, 77-2, 77-3, 77-4 and 77-5 all came up for second reading. Motions were made to pass each ordinance separately and seconded, with all voting in favor.

The Cowboy Days celebration was held during the Labor Day weekend and was reported to be a big success with very little trouble.

Chief Harvey stated that with the extra help from the Sheriff's Department and the Evanston Police Reserve Unit everything seemed to stay pretty calm. According to the Cowboy Days Committee the event, including the parade, turned out to be a big success and everyone enjoyed themselves.

During the regular council meeting on October 5th we passed on several resolutions. One of those resolutions was to authorize the city to donate $5,000 to the Wyoming State Bar Association VEHAR Reward Fund. This fund would be held for one year by the association and would be part of the reward money paid to anyone that could offer information that would lead to the arrest and conviction of those responsible for the Vehar bombing.

Resolution 77-6 established the days and times for hours of operation of the City of Evanston landfill. Other resolutions pertained to requests for grants. All resolutions introduced during the meeting passed with all voting in favor.

The subject of cleaning up the old city dumps came up for discussion. Jay and Garry Ellingford stated that the old dumps bordered their property and requested that it be cleaned up as soon as possible. During the discussion they made an offer to clean the property up at no charge if the city would donate the property to them. The council said they were not interested in selling the real estate and that someone had already offered to clean it up for the salvage. Attorney Lancaster informed the council that to sell the property, by law, it would have to be put out for bid.

Marvin Bollschweiler, representing the LDS Church, was present at the meeting to offer the Almy Cemetery to the city as a Memorial Park. The council asked about the records and how much burial space was still available. Mr. Bollschweiler said he would try to have this information available at the next city council meeting.

Ordinance 77-1 and Ordinance 77-3 came up for third and final reading. Motion was made and seconded by the council members Fruits and me, respectively, and seconded by me and Bills, respectively. Both ordinances were voted on with all voting in favor. Mayor South abstained from voting on Ordinance 77-1, because it included a pay raise for the mayor, but if it passed the pay raises would not go into effect until the mayor or council ran for re-election and won, so I don't know why he would have to abstain. Maybe it just made him feel better.

Ordinance 77-6 was introduced by Councilman Bills. This was an ordinance changing the name of 21st Street to Birch Street, changing the name of Gravel Road to Red Mountain Road, and directing the city engineer to change the city map to reflect these changes and repealing any and all conflicting ordinances.

A motion to pass this ordinance on first reading was made by Bills and seconded by me, with all voting in favor.

Mayor South called for a special meeting to be held on October 17th to pass on Resolution 77-9. This resolution was to authorize the mayor and city council to apply to the Wyoming Farm Loan Board for a Government Royalty Impact Assistance Account Grant.

The resolution was introduced by Councilman Albrecht, and read in full by Attorney Lancaster. After a short discussion it was moved for adoption by me, and seconded by Davis, with all voting in favor.

The Wyoming Highway Department called for a public meeting to get input on the construction of a new overpass off Front Street to what is now Bear River Drive. At the time of this meeting the highway through town was still called U.S. Highway 30 S, and because of an expectedly large public turnout, the meeting was held at the Uinta County Court House.

The Highway Department explained that there were plans to construct another route across the railroad and possibly the Bear River. They had four proposed routes to present in hopes of getting some input from the people of Evanston.

The four proposals were marked A, B, C and D. Proposal A would come off Front Street at the intersection of 11th Street. The route would be an overpass going over the railroad tracks and the river, ending up on Bear River Drive (formerly U.S. Highway 30 S) near the Uinta County Fairgrounds.

Proposal B would also come off 11th Street, but would end up where the intersection of Bear River Drive and the new State Highway

89 is at the present. Proposal C would come off 9th Street where the underpass already is and meet Bear River Drive about the same location as Proposal B. Proposal D would come off 6th Street and extend the overpass to the same location as Proposals B and C show.

The meeting was quite lengthy and there seemed to be a lot of interest and some input from the public, but most preferred Proposal D, off 6th Street. The representatives from the highway department thanked everyone and said that they will be working on the project, but it would probably be a few years before anything happened, because of funding.

A notice in the Uinta County Herald read; *City Clerk Don Welling reports that the regular City Council meeting scheduled for Wednesday, November 2nd will be postponed until Wednesday, November 9th at 6:00 p.m. He stated that it would be held in the council chambers of the Evanston City Hall, and that this will be an open meeting and the public is invited to attend.* I don't recall why the meeting was postponed, but Mayor South or someone must have had a good reason for it. On November 9th Mayor South opened the meeting at 6:00 p.m. as expected. After the regular business was taken care of, Ordinance 77-5, changing the dates when liquor licenses were due, came up for third and final reading.

A motion was made by me and seconded by Councilman Albrecht, all voting in favor.

Ordinance 77-2 came up for third and final reading with a motion by Councilman Bills, seconded by Fruits. A lengthy discussion was held, mostly because of some unanswered questions about the terms and conditions within the ordinance. Therefore, I made a motion to table the ordinance on the third and final reading until the next regular meeting, which was seconded by Albrecht, all voting in favor.

Ordinance 77-4 came up for second reading with a motion by Councilman Bills, seconded by Albrecht, all voting in favor. Ordinance 77-4 was an ordinance to adopt a master street plan for the northeast area of Evanston. The third and final reading was acted upon and passed during the regular meeting in December.

Ordinance 77-6, an ordinance changing street names, came up for second reading. Motion was made by me to pass Ordinance 77-6 on second reading, seconded by Councilman Fruits, all voting in favor. The third and final reading was also acted upon and passed during the regular meeting in December.

The employees' Christmas dinner came up for discussion. I made a motion that all full-time employees be paid a Christmas bonus in the amount of $25.00 each at the dinner. The motion was seconded and passed.

A special meeting was called by Mayor South on November 11th to begin at 12:00 noon. The purpose of the meeting was to discuss the bids received for a new garbage collection unit. After a short discussion, Councilman Albrecht made a motion to award the bid to the low bidder. Reese Pontiac, Cadillac and G.M.C.s bid $42,134.85, which was the low bid. The motion was seconded by Councilman Bills, and all voted in favor.

The only other business was a motion made by me to permit Mayor South to sign an agreement with Utah Power and Light Company to furnish power to the new city hall located at 12th Street and Main. The motion was seconded by Councilman Albrecht, and all voted in favor.

The regular meeting of December 7th was called to order by Mayor South at 6:00 p.m. After motions to approve the previous minutes and the payment of outstanding bills were seconded, with all voting in favor, Ordinance 77-2, that was tabled during the last meeting, came up for third and final reading. The motion was made by Councilman Bills, seconded by Rice, with all voting in favor. This ordinance pertained to subdivisions and required an owner of the land being subdivided to pay either 5% of the raw value of the land, or deed 5% of the land to the city for park and recreation purposes.

Ordinance 77-2 was later vetoed by Mayor South during the first meeting in January, 1978.

Other business that came before the council was a resolution presented to the council by Assistant Chief Chisholm and introduced by Councilman Fruits. This was Resolution 77-10 authorizing the city to apply to the Wyoming Farm Loan Board for the acquisition of police vehicles. A motion to adopt this resolution was made by Councilman Albrecht, and seconded by Davis. After a short discussion, all voted in favor.

A letter from the Masonic Cemetery Association was read by the mayor, donating $150.00 to the Evanston Cemetery Perpetual Care Fund. The mayor and council expressed a special thanks to the Masonic Organization for the donation.

The police reports from Chief Harvey for the past few months had been indicating that there was definitely a growing problem for the officers. According to police officials, the department was facing critical problems as a result of energy-development-related growth.

Officials said there had been a 30% increase in activity over the past year. A recent mid-week report showed the night shift making twelve arrests, investigating a burglary, and being called to a suicide site. They also stated that the investigator's caseload for the month of October included 96 new cases, and this did not include cases carried over from previous months.

The mayor stated that until our tax base caught up with the population growth, we were going to continue having problems, because more people always bring more problems. He went on to say that we will be hiring new officers as our budget allows, but it isn't just police problems, it's also other problems such as housing and infrastructure that we are trying to keep up with. All we can do is the best with what we have, he stated.

The oil and gas drilling didn't seem to be slacking off at all; if anything it was growing more and more each month. There was no doubt now that Evanston and Uinta County were facing an enormous boom period and all we could do is try to keep it under control and keep up with all the additional needs involved with growth.

1977 was a crazy weather year throughout America. At that time it would be known nationally *as the year the weather went haywire.* The west had one of the worst drought years in recorded history, the south and southeast were faced with some snow and a bitter cold winter causing them to lose millions in citrus fruit and vegetable production, plus a tremendous loss in the tourism industry, and the northeast had a very wet year of snow and rain. The strange pattern of weather in 1977 cost the nation several billion dollars. It was, indeed, the year that the weather went haywire.

However, Evanston had a very busy year trying to keep up with the growth and water shortage from the drought. Mayor South and his administration did a great job keeping up with all the problems, but the Vehar bombing was really depressing for all of us, especially the mayor. He didn't ever seem to get over what he had seen when he visited the site. It was an incident that should never have happened, losing three good people.

CHAPTER 12

1978....At the first regular meeting of 1978 on January 4th, Al Pilch presented the City of Evanston with a check in the amount of $7,589.67 to help finish off golf course projects such as the archery range, the driving range, some site improvements, fencing and engineering. This would be the final payment from the Wyoming Recreation Commission through the Wyoming Land and Water Conservation Fund Act.

Mayor South, in accepting the check, thanked Al Pilch for the check and for all the support he had given Evanston in the past. The city still had applications pending to request funding from the commission for other recreation and park projects, and we hoped that they would be approved.

During this meeting Mayor South vetoed Ordinance 77-2, which was an ordinance requesting all property owners that were in the process of subdividing to pay to the city 5% of the land value, or convey to the city 5% of the land for park and recreation purposes.

This was a surprise to some, but South had talked to me and some of the other council members regarding his intentions. I suggested to him that he may have a conflict of interest because his company, South and Jones, had been and was involved in a subdivision. Therefore, I was not in agreement with him at the time, but I did suggest to him to talk to the attorney about his conflict. He said, *I have already talked to the attorney and he told me to use my own judgment because I was mayor. So,* he said, half pissed off, *I am going to do just that and the veto will stand.*

The mayor explained to me that there were a few things in the ordinance that needed to be corrected and said he would veto this ordinance so it could be corrected. One of the important items in the ordinance that needed to be acted on was the 5% land value and how the value was to be determined. The provision of both parties having the right to have the land appraised to determine a fair value was incorporated into the new ordinance, among a few other changes. Although he was probably right, I still voted against the veto, because I thought a better way to correct the ordinance would have been through amendments, but in the end it didn't matter because it all came out okay.

When the mayor called for the veto, Councilman Jimmie Rice moved to override the veto, and was seconded by Fruits. After a short discussion South called for a roll call vote with Albrecht voting no; Rice, yes; Fruits, yes; Bills, no; Davis no; and me, yes. The motion failed with a tied vote of 3 in favor and 3 against. Mayor South's veto still held and Ordinance 77-2 was no longer in effect, but an ordinance to replace it would come up in February.

Councilman Roy Fruits introduced Resolution 77-13, a resolution authorizing the city to go into a lease/purchase agreement to acquire a loader. The motion to adopt was made by Fruits, seconded by Albrecht, with all voting in favor.

During the meeting Mayor South appointed retired Lieutenant Leonard Wold, formerly of the Wyoming Highway Patrol, to the position of City Judge. Wold had been on the highway patrol for quite some time. At the time of his retirement he was commander of a region in Western Wyoming. He and his wife Marie had lived in Evanston raising their family all those years. So he was no stranger to the area and its problems.

Sam Corson, an Evanston Attorney for many, many years had previously held the position of City Judge and was getting up in years, so he submitted his letter of resignation. The mayor and council accepted it with their appreciation for the service he had given.

Chief Dennis Harvey made his report and said that the city is advertising in the Uinta County Herald for more reserve police officers with a headline stating, RESERVE POLICE OFFICERS NEEDED.

Mayor South called for a special meeting to be held on January 25th at 6:00 p.m. to open bids for drilling of water wells. He made a special effort to let the public know that they were invited.

The Herald's issue dated January 19th had an article titled MOUNTAIN FUEL WILL CONSTRUCT A GAS PROCESSING PLANT. The plant would be located in the Butcher Knife Springs field in Uinta County. The article went on to say that the plant will remove hydrogen sulfide (H2S) and carbon dioxide from natural gas and condensate. This is necessary before product can be transported through pipelines or marketed. Construction was scheduled to begin February 15th, and it would take about one year to complete. Cost will be about seven million dollars, and this plant would serve Southwestern Wyoming and Utah.

The special meeting of January 25th, previously announced by the mayor, was to open bids for drilling water wells. However, no bids had been received. Mr. Eric Hawkinson from the Farmer's Home Administration (FHA) said that as no bids were received after properly advertising, that the city, by rights, could find a local driller and negotiate with him on the cost to drill a well.

It came to the attention of the mayor and council that helicopters from C. G. Geophysical and Rocky Mountain Helicopter Services had been landing their units in areas not zoned for it. City Attorney Lancaster explained he didn't think that the ordinance had any provision in it concerning helicopters and areas where they could land in the city. Mayor South directed Lancaster to look into it and prepare an amendment or ordinance allowing certain zones they can use for landing. Occasionally there might be emergencies where helicopters need to land right now, and neither the hospital nor the city had a landing site for them. The nearest location would be the airport, which were several miles north of Evanston. With the way the city's growing there is no doubt that there is definitely a need for a helicopter landing site.

The Uinta County Herald came out with an issue on February 9th with a headline that read JUDGE SAYS GAMBLING CHARGE NOT VALID. The article went on to say that District Judge C. Stuart Brown expressed his opinion that the eight Uinta County men arrested last June 22nd on a gambling charge should not be punished criminally.

He said, rather, that, *The court holds that it was not the intent of Section 6-203 W.S. 1957, to make it a crime to play a casual game of poker for money or other representatives of value in a private residence or office when the public is excluded.* Therefore the case was dropped.

The Herald issue of February 16th had an article titled NEW AERIAL LADDER TRUCK ARRIVES. It stated that the Evanston Volunteer Fire Department accepted delivery of the new truck Thursday, February 9th. Fire Chief Jerry Cazin said, *This is a piece of equipment with a 65 foot aerial ladder that is badly needed because of the growth and the higher building structures, and that the department was very grateful to receive the truck during the department's 92nd anniversary year.*

Mayor South, on behalf of the council, congratulated the fire department for their 92 years of service to the community and surrounding areas, and thanked them for being available when needed.

During our regular council meeting on February 8th, Traffic Committee Chairman John Deru and member Rick Sather reported their findings. This committee was appointed by the mayor months ago with the idea of studying the traffic and parking problems in downtown Evanston. They stated that they would present the committee's plans of alternate traffic patterns with proposals for one way traffic on the downtown streets at a public meeting on March 2nd at 7:00 p.m. at the Uinta County Courthouse. These plans would be posted for everyone to be able to study at that meeting.

Mayor South thanked them for their hard work and stated that the traffic problem was getting worse all the time, mainly because of the bottleneck at the underpass, and something had to be done to improve the problem.

The Herald, in the same February 16th issue, had an article with the title TRAFFIC COMMITTEE PROPOSES ONE WAY TRAFFIC IN DOWNTOWN. It made the announcement that on March 2nd residents of Evanston would have the opportunity to speak their minds concerning traffic problems in the downtown area at a 7:00 p.m. hearing at the Uinta County Courthouse. The alternate plans for traffic would be on display at the meeting.

During the meeting, Mr. Deru and Mr. Sather presented alternate plans for traffic flow on one way streets. They talked about the plan that the committee favored, and that diagonal parking would be on Main and Center Streets. They also recommended that the city provide and improve two parking lots in the downtown area, but after a considerable amount of discussion, there seemed to be some objection from the public, especially downtown merchants, of what the direction of the flow of traffic would be and whether the parking would be adequate. Therefore, there was no decision made during that meeting.

Mr. Steve Snyder, representing LUAG, was at our regular council meeting of February 8th to present a master plan for the City of Evanston. He requested that the mayor and council call for a workshop meeting on February 23rd at 7:00 p.m. to go over the proposed master plan, and then call for a public hearing to be held at city hall March 21st. Mayor South and the council concurred with Snyder's request.

Resolution 78-1, introduced by Councilman David Bills, came up for discussion. This was a resolution to annex Red Mountain Terrace, requested by a partnership of properties. After a short discussion it was moved by me and seconded by Fruits. The motion passed with five yes votes. Both Fife and South abstained, because of their ownership of some property included in the annexation.

During this same meeting Mayor South received a letter from Leonard Wold who was resigning as City Judge. Wold had just been appointed a month or so ago. Why he resigned so quickly I don't recall, but in accepting his letter Mayor South appointed Steve Aaron to fill the vacancy. Councilman Bills moved to confirm the appointment of Aaron as City Judge, seconded by Fruits, with all voting in favor.

During the February 8th meeting, Councilman Bills introduced Ordinance 78-1. This ordinance would replace Ordinance 77-2, which Mayor South had vetoed in January.

Ordinance 78-1 would be an ordinance to amend and re-enact section 19-16 (d) (e) (f) of the revised code of the City of Evanston,

Wyoming 1977, providing for conveyance of land to the city for parks and recreation purposes, or at the option of the city, in lieu of such conveyance of land, to pay to the city a cash amount, by establishing a special fund for such payment.

It was intended to be passed on an emergency; therefore it was moved by Fruits to suspend the rules, seconded by Rice, but the motion died with all voting against it.

The motion to pass Ordinance 78-1 on first reading was made by Fruits and seconded by Rice, with all voting in favor.

Resolution 78-2 was introduced by me. This resolution authorized the city clerk to repay the owners of the M Bar B Subdivision for additional costs incurred by the owners for hooking onto the north sewer line rather than the south sewer line, which was adjacent to their property. Apparently this was a mistake by the city directing the owner to hook up at the wrong location. The motion for adoption was made by Fruits and seconded by Davis, all voting in favor.

City Attorney Lancaster presented several agreements with FHA relative to the city receiving a grant to drill two new water wells. A motion to accept the grant was made by me, and seconded by Fruits, with all voting in favor.

Additionally, during the meeting, Resolution 78-3 was introduced by me, authorizing the mayor and city clerk to enter into an agreement with MCO Drilling, Inc. for the drilling of the water wells for the city.

It was moved by Bills to adopt Resolution 78-3, seconded by Davis, all voting in favor.

The February 23rd issue of the Uinta County Herald had an article titled PARKING PROPOSAL AIRED. It went on to say that the local citizens would have the opportunity to hear the proposed downtown parking changes and the proposed one-way street routes and to ask questions on Friday, February 24th at 7:00 p.m. on Cable TV and KEVA Radio. Mayor South and representatives of his downtown parking and traffic committee would present the proposals and the public would have the opportunity to make telephone calls with questions concerning proposals.

This was the first time that the cable company and the radio station had been used for this type of public service, and it turned out to be a very successful way of reaching out to the public concerning city issues.

Also, the special public meeting scheduled for Thursday, March 3rd at 7:00 p.m. was held at the Uinta County Courthouse for those interested citizens to be heard concerning the downtown traffic and parking problems. The meeting was poorly attended; a few downtown business people were all that showed up. At that time there was still no decision made concerning any of the proposals. It would be a year or so before any changes would be in effect.

Amoco Production Company made the announcement in the local paper that they were scheduling eight new test wells in the Ryckman Creek field just northwest of Evanston. It was stated that the wells would go from 7,850 feet to 8,300 feet for testing the Nugget foundation.

It was reported by the Petroleum Information Corp. that through October 1977, the last month for which complete statistics were available, the Overthrust Belt field's eight completed wells had produced more than 300,000 barrels of oil. Daily field average from the wells currently in production was 2,320 barrels.

It was announced in the March 9th issue of the Herald, SIXTH STREET TO BE NEW HIGHWAY TOUCHDOWN POINT. The announcement came from the Wyoming Highway Department, but it would still be another four or five years before funds were available for the completion.

Most of the folks who lived on Sixth Street were quite unhappy about the choice, because it was bound to cause a lot of additional traffic. A group of them requested that the city hold an election to determine what route the public favored. The city attorney was directed to look into this and get back to the council.

At the regular meeting of the city council on March 8th, there was a motion made and passed to recess with the Joint Powers Board to open and discuss bids on another phase of the water project. No action was taken on the bids at that time.

The council reconvened and opened bids on the sewer cleaning equipment that the city had advertised for. There were only two bids. The first bid was from the Triple C Distributing Company of Wyoming for $7,370. The other bid was from Cannon Sales of Illinois for $6,555 F.O.B.

Councilman Fruits made a motion to take this matter under advisement with consideration of the 5% differential under Wyoming law concerning in-state bidders and out-of-state bidders, and then awarded the bid to the low bidder, seconded by me, all voting in favor.

Ordinance 78-1, where the landowner of a subdivision was required to either convey 5% of the land to the city for park and recreation purposes, or pay 5% in cash of the raw land value in lieu, came up for a second reading. The motion was made by Bills, seconded by me, with all voting in favor.

Ordinance 78-2, to allow helicopter landing ports in C-3 and I-1 zones, came up for a second reading. After a short discussion, Councilman Davis moved for passage on second reading, seconded by Albrecht, with all voting in favor.

Both Ordinances, 78-1 and 78-2, were moved, seconded and passed on third and final reading during the regular meeting held on April 5th, with all voting in favor.

During the regular meeting of March 8th Ordinance 78-3, to annex 80.57 acres of Section 16, Township 15 North, Range 120 West, of Uinta County, was introduced by Councilman Albrecht. It was moved by Bills to pass on first reading, and seconded by me, with all voting in favor.

Ordinance 78-3 came up for a second reading during the March 28th meeting, and passed with all voting in favor. Also, the ordinance came up for vote on the third and final reading during the regular meeting of April 5th with all voting in favor.

Chief Harvey gave his report, which included the same old problems: dogs, traffic, bar problems, and so on. The reason we were starting to have problems in the bars was because they were becoming overcrowded from the fast population growth we were experiencing. By state law and by population, a city could only have a certain number of liquor licenses. The city controlled the licenses, while the state controlled how many, based on population. The next time Evanston could or would be eligible to apply for additional licenses would be based on the 1980 census, which would take a couple more years. This would cause Evanston and the police department a lot of problems in the meantime.

Also, Councilman Davis suggested that an officer walking in the downtown area would be a good move for the department and city. The mayor and council all agreed with Davis and Chief Harvey initiated the idea.

City Attorney Lancaster announced to the council that there would not be an election to determine which route the proposed overpass would use. A number of citizens wanted to put the four proposals up for election, but the law did not require it and the mayor and city council did not feel that it would be necessary, due to lack of funds. Therefore, the Wyoming Highway Department's decision to use 6th Street would be the route whenever the state had the funds available.

City Engineer John Proffit made his report on the new water drilling operation at the cemetery and presented a preliminary plat of some new cemetery lots, and Superintendent of Public Works Allen Kennedy reported about the difficult time they were having cleaning the streets with all the cars, trucks and trailers that are either never or very seldom moved. He said that the street department would probably have the same problem with snow removal in the wintertime.

Mayor South reported that a public hearing was held pertaining to the Evanston master plan on March 28th, but there was not much accomplished at the time. However, those in attendance felt good about the fact that the city was trying to make an effort to better the community. The master plan would come up at a later date, because it was very important that the city had a plan to help control the fast growth Evanston was now facing.

A new article was published in the Uinta County Herald issue of March 30th titled GAS DISCOVERY REPORTED NORTHEAST OF COALVILLE. The article went on to describe a gas discovery capable of flowing 3 million cubic feet per day, located about 14 miles northeast of Coalville, Utah on the Anschultz Ranch Company of Denver, Colorado. The ranch was located mostly in Utah but it overlapped into Wyoming southwest of Evanston a dozen miles or so.

The paper also stated that a new population projection made by LUAG showed that they had found a significant increase of population in Uinta County and Evanston since the 1970 census, but the report didn't seem to help much in state funding or liquor licenses.

A news article came out in an April issue of the Herald that another oil/gas well was completed by Chevron northeast of Evanston. It seemed that about every week you would read in the paper about another oil or gas discovery in the area. The area was growing fast and Evanston and Uinta County were having some real problems from it.

Another news article in the April issue said that the Overthrust Belt region may be the most important and largest oil and gas discovery the country has seen in the last twenty years. It was such a big discovery that the federal government and their agencies got involved. It was reported that the discovery was being hampered by federal restrictions, but at this point it didn't seem to slow things down any.

Also, it was reported that the area snow fall was about normal from the past winter, and that we might not have to ration water during the summer, but the city would be watching it very closely.

During the April meeting the council adopted Resolution 78-8, introduced by Councilman Albrecht, waiving the monthly charge for water, sewer and garbage service for the Uinta County Senior Citizens Center located in Evanston, from July 1, 1978 through June 30, 1979. It was moved and seconded for adoption with all voting in favor.

Mr. Steve Snyder, a representative of LUAG, presented a resolution which was introduced by Councilman Albrecht. This Resolution 78-10 authorized the mayor to sign a community development block grant application with the U.S. Department of HUD and with the state clearinghouse. It was moved and seconded for adoption with all voting in favor.

A special city council meeting was held on April 12th to open bids for the furnishings of the new police justice building and city hall. The city received several bids; therefore there was a group of interested bidders present at the meeting. The bids were opened and read by Erin Muth, one of the architects, and after a short discussion the mayor turned them over to Muth to tabulate the bids, check specifications and funding, and so on, and make recommendations for awarding of the furnishing bids at a special meeting to be held on April 25th.

The only other business to come before the council during the April 12th meeting was Mayor South reading a letter from Nebeker Oil Company about withdrawing their bid for fuel. Why they withdrew their bid I don't recall, but at that time the city was purchasing fuel from local distributors and each year they would ask for bids. Also during the meeting the parking and traffic problems were once again discussed, but nothing was accomplished at that time.

On April 7th, the city and counties finally received their revenue-sharing checks from the State of Wyoming. These were funds that the various entities had been hoping and waiting for the past few months. Evanston received $218,187 of the funds.

In the first part of May, Evanston finally received their new garbage disposal truck. Mayor South congratulated Verdon Moore, foreman of the sanitary department, and Allen Kennedy, Superintendent of Public Works, and told them that the new truck will be a big help to the department. Moore said that the new truck was something that the department had been in need of for a long, long time, and that it would make the job much easier and faster.

During our regular meeting of May 3rd, we took care of business as usual, plus we adopted Resolution 78-11, pertaining to the vacating of certain streets that were affected by the new Interstate 80 and the old Lincoln Highway (U.S. Highway 30 S). We followed that with Ordinance 78-5, also pertaining to the vacating of the same streets that had been on the previous plat of the City of Evanston.

This ordinance was introduced and over a couple more meetings was passed on first, second and third readings with all voting in favor.

The purpose of the ordinance was merely to correct the city's boundaries because of the new freeway and the highway department's changes to old Lincoln Highway.

Also during the May meeting, a day care center came under discussion and consideration. Although there were a few small private day care facilities available, there didn't seem to be enough to fill the need. A lot of mothers who were holding down jobs, especially single mothers, were having problems finding places to leave their children. Because of the availability of jobs and the increase in population from what was starting to be a big oil and gas boom, this was getting to be a big problem. At this time the city did not do anything except try to encourage more private centers to become available, but laws concerning day care centers were becoming pretty strict. This discouraged some people from going into this type of business.

During discussion there were suggestions made about the city getting involved and opening up a public day care center that would handle a large number of children while their mothers worked, but it was a few more years before the city opened up the center, which would eventually be called the Evanston Child Development Center (E.C.D.C.).

Mayor South called for a special meeting on May 9th to take care of more pressing business including Ordinance 78-6, pertaining to amending some of the problems we were having concerning Highway Commercial C-1 zoning and deleting Mobile Home Parks from just a permitted use permit, and requiring them to obtain a conditional use permit. This ordinance was introduced and also pasted on the three readings with all voting in favor.

Mayor South also called for a special meeting on May 12th. This meeting was called for the purpose of passing Resolution 78-12 directing the mayor and city clerk to apply to the Wyoming State Loan Board for a coal tax grant. The resolution was introduced and adopted with all voting in favor.

With more oil and gas wells going up in the area and the fast increase in population, problems for the city, county and school district were getting more and more pressing. However, we were doing the best we could under the circumstances. We were getting some assistance in funding from various state agencies and commissions, but were looking forward to the time when the tax revenues began catching up with the problems. But it was getting tough and a lot of folks were getting a little worried.

At our regular meeting of June 12th, which was postponed for a week at the request of the mayor, Miss Margaret Smith once again was in attendance. I believe this made the council a little nervous, including me, but the mayor knew exactly why she was there.

She seemed to be having some problems with getting water to her house which was set back off of County Road. Her water line apparently had to be changed because it was coming from other homes and not off the main. She knew this and agreed to get it corrected.

Mayor South assured her that the city would do whatever they had to do to assist in correcting the situation, but some of the cost would be at her expense. She was very good about the situation and assured us that she would do whatever she had to do to get it corrected. The mayor also assured her that the city would locate a good contractor to get the job done.

Other business that came up during the June meeting included passing on various ordinances and resolutions, and Dennis Poppinga, Recreation Director, gave a written report to the council on activities concerning his department.

LUAG gave a report and asked for some funding from the city. They requested funding for two items: $5,700 for one item and $1,800 for the other. Mayor South suggested that the council support this request. Therefore a resolution was introduced with a motion and second to adopt, all voting in favor.

In Chief Harvey's report he recommended that the City of Evanston join the National Law Officers Institute. The motion was made and seconded, with all voting in favor.

Also in attendance was Mr. Joe Fessenden, representing the Uinta County Memorial Hospital located on Uinta Street between 12th and 13th Streets. He asked permission from the city to use the intersection of 12th and Uinta for a landing pad for helicopters when needed.

It was explained that there could be some safety problems, but Fessenden assured us that safety preparations would be made prior to any landings or take-offs. A motion to temporarily allow the hospital to use the site for emergency helicopter landings was made and seconded. All voted in favor.

In other business, it was suggested that Allen Kennedy, Superintendent of Public Works, attend a seminar on landfills in Jackson, and Butch Whittaker and Robert Tueller of the water department made their report on a water training school that they had recently attended. It was reported that Whittaker had successfully obtained his "B" Operator Certification and Tueller had received his "D" Operator Certification as a result of recent tests taken.

At the request of the mayor, I made a motion to postpone the next regular meeting in July to the 12th rather than July 5th, seconded by Albrecht with all voting in favor.

Mayor South also called for a special meeting on June 15th for the purpose of a public hearing concerning an overrun on the engineer's estimate on a water project that was being funded by the Wyoming Farm Loan Board. After a lengthy discussion was held by the council, a public hearing on the proposed Revenue Sharing Budget was held at 7:30 p.m.

Apparently the engineer's estimate was short approximately $60,000, and the hearing was held for the purpose of allowing the mayor and city clerk to transfer funds from the budget while the city applied for additional funding from the Wyoming Farm Loan Board. Motions were made and seconded to accept the preliminary budget, and to apply for more funding from the Revenue Sharing Budget of the Farm Loan Board. All voted in favor.

During this meeting we also wrote a new job description for Bill George, Building Inspector, stating that part of his job was to be secretary to the Planning and Zoning Commission, with a $100.00 increase in pay. The motion was made and seconded, with all voting in favor.

I was appointed as the liaison to the Day Care Center Committee by the mayor and council. On May 4th, the Uinta County Herald issue had two articles concerning the committee. One article was titled DAY CARE CENTER COMMITTEE ASKS CITY FOR BUILDING SITE; the other was DAY CARE CENTER COMM. PLANS TO INCORPORATE.

A few years later the city allowed the day care center to lease two subdivided lots off of the Railroad Park property near the North Elementary School. The city also furnished the center with two modular type buildings and hooked up the buildings with all utilities. This is when they named the center the Evanston Child Development Center (E.C.D.C.).

The second news article that concerned the Day Care Center Committee's plans of incorporating didn't happen for a couple more years, not until they changed the name. In the meantime, the committee proceeded with their plans for the facility and programs for the children. They were planning on a center that could take care of approximately 50 children, with kitchen facilities and all. The only thing holding them back was finding the right location and the funding to get things started.

Also in May the Wyoming Farm Loan Board approved a grant in the amount of $100,000 to Evanston to pay the costs of relocating a state-owned bridge from Wyoming State Highway 89 near the old airport to North Evanston. The two-lane bridge was to replace the old one-lane over Bear River on Holland Drive that had been a problem for the public for a long time. With the one-lane bridge, a vehicle going one way would have to stop and wait for the opposite vehicle to cross the bridge before it could cross.

During the special meeting of June 28th, after my meeting with the Uinta County Commissioners and the Memorial Hospital Board, I reported to the mayor and council that the property at the top of 10th Street, where Davis Middle School is now located, had been freed from any commitments to the county, and that it had been determined that the City of Evanston is legal owner. The previous doubt of ownership had now been cleared up.

During the meeting a group of citizens representing the proposed Day Care Center Committee presented to the council some preliminary plans and answered several questions. After a lengthy discussion I made a motion to give the mayor approval to work with the city attorney to draw up a lease agreement on a proposed site for a day care center, with this agreement to be presented at the regular meeting on July 12th and subject to the council's approval. It was seconded by Bills. After a short discussion a vote was called with all voting in favor.

Cloey Wall, of Uinta Engineering and Surveying, presented a proposed plat and a petition for annexation of 90+ acres of the Uinta Downs property located just south of Interstate 80 and east of Yellow Creek Road.

Mr. Wall introduced Mr. Doyle Child of Holback Realty of Afton, Wyoming as the new owner of the Uinta Downs property, and indicated that he was representing Mr. Child pertaining to the proposed plat and the petition for annexation.

After a question and answer period, Resolution 78-15 was introduced by me for the annexation of the 90+ acres of land to be included in the City of Evanston. Motion was made by Davis to adopt resolution, seconded by Rice, with all voting in favor.

At the end of the meeting I brought up the issue of passenger train service in Wyoming provided by Amtrak, and the fact that the state could lose this service. I stated that Governor Ed Herschler had announced that a representative of the U.S. Office of Rail Public Council had conducted public meetings in Cheyenne on June 26th in preparation for an Interstate Commerce Commission hearing on July 12th regarding possible termination of Amtrak passenger train service across Southern Wyoming, which would include all cities from Cheyenne to Evanston.

After a short discussion on the subject I made a statement in the form of a motion that the mayor and city council attend the meeting, and speak in favor of retaining the services of Amtrak in the State of Wyoming. The motion was seconded by Rice with all voting in favor.

There was an article in the Uinta County Herald titled NAT'L ATTENTION ON UTAH-WYO. DRILLING FRONTIER,

indicating that the Overthrust Belt frontier was getting more national attention than ever before. New Nugget formation test wells
were scheduled in the Evanston region, and several significant deep
wells were at critical depths. The article said that the oil and gas industry were paying particular attention to developments along the
Overthrust Belt area, and it went on to say that it was certainly one
of the most important exploratory events in the U.S. in many years.

It appeared that Evanston was in for a big economic boom that
would cause a lot of growing problems, which it already had, but it
also appeared that the oil and gas industry and the state of Wyoming
were willing to help us try to keep up.

During the regular city council meeting held on July 12th Councilman Albrecht introduced Ordinance 78-11, pertaining to the
annexation of the 90+ acres mentioned in Resolution 78-15 and
requested by the new owner, Mr. Doyle Child. Section 9 of the ordinance deemed that an emergency existed. Councilman Davis moved
to suspend the rules and pass Ordinance 78-11 on an emergency basis,
seconded by Fruits. The motion was passed with at least three-fourths
voting in favor.

Councilman Fruits then made the motion to pass the ordinance
on an emergency basis, seconded by me with all voting in favor.

Other business that came up during the meeting included several public hearings about zone changes throughout various areas of
Evanston, and Charles Albrecht, Surveyor, presented a new plat for
Aspen Grove II, a new proposed subdivision. It was moved and seconded for approval with all voting in favor.

Kilburn Porter presented a preliminary plat for Porters Subdivision, which would be located out of the city limits, but adjacent to the
city. A discussion pursuant to this new subdivision took place.

The mayor and city council expressed a desire for this proposed
subdivision to be annexed, as it was contiguous to the city, in order
for it to be approved. The city had jurisdiction, at that time, of one
half mile outside the limits of the city.

Just before the mayor called for the recess, Don Welling, City
Clerk, reminded everyone that the filing dates for running for office

for the 1978 election were from July 14th through July 28th and that the Primary Election was going to be held on September 12th.

Mayor South then recessed the meeting at 11:40 p.m. until July 18th at 6:00 p.m. at which time it would reconvene.

At the meeting of July 18th, a continuance of the previous regular meeting of July 12th was opened by Mayor South at 6:12 p.m. During this meeting, residential plats of Uinta Downs were presented by Mr. Child and Cloey Wall, Surveyor. The plats were accepted by motion and seconded, with all voting in favor.

In other business there were public hearing requests by a few property owners, with no action taken at this time. Some zone change requests were approved, and one was tabled until the next regular meeting. A conditional use permit was denied and recommended that it go back to the Planning and Zoning Commission to go through the proper procedure before it was presented to the council again. In addition to the business on hand at the meeting there were a couple of ordinances introduced, mostly amendments to previous ordinances, and successfully accepted and approved. Also, there were two resolutions introduced concerning the Evanston Joint Powers Board and the Southwestern Wyoming Water Quality Planning Association. Both resolutions were accepted with all voting in favor.

At 8:00 p.m. of this meeting, a public hearing was called for the proposed City Budget and Revenue Sharing Fund for the fiscal year of 1978-1979. The hearing was short because of lack of interest. There was no one present at the hearing who had any questions. Therefore, Mayor South stated that this public hearing had been properly and legally advertised, but with no questions or concerns it would be officially closed.

He called for a meeting the next day on July 19th at 12:00 noon to act on the budget. Therefore, I made the motion to approve the budget as presented in the public hearing held on July 18th, seconded by Davis. The motion passed with all voting in favor.

The resolution was introduced by Councilman Fruits that on the 18th day of July, 1978 the budget making authority prepared and submitted to the council a city budget for the fiscal year ending

June 30, 1979. The resolution was moved and seconded for adoption with all voting in favor.

During Bob Burns' second term as mayor, the Greater Evanston Development Company (G.E.D.C.) turned the lease of the Wyoming Railway Car Company over to the city with a new lease. There were no changes in the lease, but due to the lack of interest in the development company at this time, I took the initiative to suggest that the lease become an agreement between the city and railway car company, and I also made the motion to do so. The motion was seconded and after a short discussion all voted in favor. To me it made more sense to have the railway car company paying the city directly as the city held the ownership of the property.

However, the money that had been received from the railway company over the few years by G.E.D.C. remained in the development company's bank account for future use, because the group did stay active and continued to try to improve the economy. I was still president and the board was still in place.

A few years ago, Colonel Oliver Shiflet sold the Wyoming Railway Car Company to a Canadian company called Lithcote Corp. I'm not sure of just when Lithcote bought Shiflet out or just when Lithcote changed to the Union Tank Car Company of Chicago, IL, the present owner.

During the meeting of July 18th, as president of the G.E.D.C., I led a discussion about a new lease agreement with the Union Tank Car Company, which had just recently taken over the car company from Lithcote Corp. I suggested that the city bring the lease up to date with no changes except an increase in the monthly rent. Union Tank did not oppose the increase because they knew that Evanston was having financial problems with the continued fast growth; and the company was very successful.

Although Lithcote was only leasing the property there was a provision in the lease agreement stating that the lessee (Lithcote Corp.)

pay the Ad Valorem taxes (property tax) on all real estate and all permanent structures in the agreement. This provision had been part of the lease from the beginning and had been over and above the monthly rental amount, and that provision helped increase both the city and county tax revenues.

Mayor Dan South directed City Attorney Lancaster to follow up with the preparation of a new lease with the suggested changes and meet with the tank company for their approval.

The Uinta County Herald reported that the No. 1 Ryckman gas/oil well was on fire. The well was located about 15 miles north of Evanston. The fire had started during the predawn hours on Sunday, July 30th, but the cause was undetermined.

"Wink" Jones, Amoco Production Coordinator, knew that the fire could not be contained by the local fire department, so they immediately called the famous Red Adair team. Red Adair and his special crews arrived with their special equipment on Sunday and Monday. The Adair team was noted for their experience in fighting oil and gas well fires, and they had the fire contained and under control by Wednesday.

Oil and gas well fires have their own personalities, Jones said. *Each one has its own characteristics that must be analyzed for best control. Once the final assessment is made, we will proceed with speed and caution. Meanwhile the company's investigation will proceed to determine the cause.*

The Uinta County Herald issue of August 3rd announced that Bob Burns, former mayor of Evanston, had been elected chairman of the Wyoming Aeronautics Commission. The action had been taken at the annual meeting of the commission recently held in Sheridan. As a member of the state commission, Burns took a big part in helping Evanston get the new airport that became a reality in a few years.

Burns had served on the commission for five years. He was originally appointed to the commission by Governor Stanley Hathaway during the time he was Mayor of the City of Evanston.

Also, in the same issue of the Herald it was announced that as of August 7th James (Buff) Bruce would have served 20 years as an employee of the City of Evanston. In all of those years he had been foreman of the Street Department.

During those 20 years, Buff had served the city under five mayors. He began with Mayor Robert Hamblin, and continued under Mayors Harold Kelly, Harold (Shorty) Raybourn, Robert (Bob) Burns and now Dan South. Buff was congratulated on his service to the city, his dependability, and his ability to accept the criticism that accompanies any public job. Although Buff had been honored for his 20 years of service to the city at this time he continued to stay on the job as the Street Foreman, until he chose to retire years later.

Before the filing dates for election which opened July 14th through July 28th I met with Mayor South and explained to him that I was planning to run for mayor this election and that I hoped that he would not be offended or have any hard feelings towards me it if he was also planning to run again for mayor. I also told him that I wanted to run last election, but when Bob Burns decided to run for re-election I held off and ran for the council again. His response kind of surprised me. He said that was okay with him because he was going to run for County Commissioner. He went on to say that his father, Ran South, had been commissioner for many years and he kind of wanted to follow in his father's footsteps. He also said that I would make a damn good mayor, and I thanked him for it.

Later on, when he was talking to Sandy, my wife, about me running for Mayor, South told her that I would probably be a better mayor than he was anyway, because I had more knowledge of the city government than he did and I had done a good job as councilman and helped him a lot during his term as mayor.

During the regular meeting of August 2nd, Mr. John "Dub" Mills presented his application, which was tabled last meeting, for a zone change from Residential to Commercial. City Attorney Lancaster and attorney Larry Lehman, representing Mills, requested it be brought back on the floor for discussion. There was opposition in attendance which included a few neighbors, Gerald "Jerry" Cazin, Robert Ball, Richard Salmela and John Proffit.

After a lengthy discussion Councilman Rice made the motion to deny Mills's request, seconded by Albrecht, with all voting in favor.

Other business during the meeting consisted of several ordinances to be introduced and considered on the first reading. Those ordinances included giving Mountain Fuel Supply Company a renewal of their franchise with the city; amending the ordinance giving the city the jurisdiction of one-half mile outside the city limits; accepting the dedication of a new street in the Red Mountain Terrace subdivision; prohibiting the parking of any vehicle in excess of two hours at any metered parking space; providing a time on the two-hour parking at metered spaces effective from 9 a.m. to 6 p.m.; providing for the establishment of no parking zones effective from 5 a.m. to 7 a.m. on designated streets; establishing the authority to remove vehicles illegally parked or for snow removal and improvement procedures; and amending and re-enacting a chapter of the revised code of the city, 1977, entitled "Zoning."

At the end of the meeting Mayor South stated that a notice would be published in the local newspaper announcing that there would be a public hearing on October 18th. This hearing would be to consider new proposed zoning matters initiated by the Evanston Planning and Zoning Commission. The meeting would be at the new administration building and would begin at 7:00 p.m.

There was more bad news when Lulu Decker, County Assessor, reported to the Uinta County Commissioners that there would be a county-wide drop in the mill levy for 1978. Unfortunately, Evanston had the largest drop in the county with a decrease of 9.24 mills, plus a Bond Sinking and Interest drop of 2.70. This report was bad news for the entire county, including all towns and school districts. All entities of the county were made aware of this early enough to adjust their budgets for the next fiscal year. The Evanston City Council did adjust their budget before the final public hearing for the fiscal year of 1978-1979, which was approved.

The Evanston School District reported a 30% increase in the kindergarten enrollment, indicating an increase throughout all grades from K-12. This caused the district a lot of concerns on how they were going to obtain the needed space for additional classrooms so that the classes were not so overcrowded, especially in the 6th, 7th and 8th grades. There was a real need for more schools and eventually new schools would be constructed, but that wasn't helping the problem at this time.

Filing dates for the election of 1978 were over, and Governor Ed Herschler was running for re-election for his second term. He would be running on the Democrat ticket against Republican Margaret McKinstry.

Those that would be running for Mayor in the primary election were me, Don Frederick and Keith W. Grover. By running for mayor, I was leaving an opening in Ward 1. Those running for councilman in Ward 1 would be Vernon E. Smith and Russell A. Megeath; for councilman of Ward 2 would be incumbent Roy M. Fruits, who would be unopposed; and for Ward 3 would be incumbent Ronald O. Davis, opposed by Miss Margaret V. Smith.

Mayor Dan South was running for County Commissioner on the Republican ticket. Others running against him on that ticket were S. Clark Anderson and Richard Sims. There were two opening for commissioner that election year so only one of the three would lose in the primary election slated for September 12th. The primary election was over, with me and Keith Grover running against each other in the mayoral race, and all those running for the council positions would all still be running in the general election. Dan South and S.Clark Anderson won on the Republican ticket for County Commissioner, and William A. Megeath and K. Wesley Davis won on the Democrat ticket.

According to the Uinta County Herald there was a good turnout for the primary election. Apparently, with the fast growth and the lack of revenue, plus all the problems we were having because of it, the voters were becoming more concerned with what was happening within the county.

Mayor South called for a special meeting on September 22nd to finalize the lease agreement with Lithcote Corp/Union Tank Car Company. County Commissioner Gene Martin was present to give a report on the present tax position in the county and stated he was in favor of a lease with Lithcote because of the tax increase and how much it would help the city and county.

A motion was made by Councilman Bills to offer a 10-year lease to Lithcote for $2,000 per month with two 10-year options and an escalation and arbitration clause. All other provisions in the lease would remain the same; insurance, taxes, and so on. The motion was seconded by me, with all voting in favor.

The representative from Union Tank Car Company verbally agreed to the lease and the mayor directed City Attorney Lancaster to draw up a resolution and lease agreement for the next meeting.

The new city hall and police justice building located on the corner of 12th and Main Streets was dedicated, and the cornerstone ceremony was at 1:00 p.m. on Saturday, September 30th. The new building contained more than 13,000 square feet of office space and meeting rooms, including a city council room that would also be used for city court. This room had the seating capacity to accommodate a large number of interested citizens and visitors. The new building was expected to be ready for the first regular city council meeting on October 4th, and it was.

The dedication was made by Mayor Dan South, and the Deputy Grand Marshall from the Masonic Grand Lodge A.F. and A.M. of Wyoming conducted the cornerstone ceremony. He was assisted by other Grand Lodge officers and the members of the Evanston Lodge #4. Also in attendance were other city, county and state officials.

On October 4th we held our first meeting at the new City Administration Building. This was our regular meeting for the month and it appeared that it was going to be a busy one. We had a large attendance of visitors and people that were interested in certain items on the agenda.

Mayor South called the meeting to order and welcomed all those in attendance. The usual business such as the approval of the minutes of the last meeting and the approval to pay the outstanding bills was taken care of by a motion and second with all voting in favor of both items of the agenda.

City Engineer John Proffit made a report on the Holland Drive bridge project. He reported that some additional land had been obtained from Dan Ellingford on the south side of the road for additional right-of-way.

Chief Jerry Cazin of the Evanston Voluntary Fire Department reported that some people were opposed to the fire department providing ambulance service for the Evanston Cowboy Days rodeo and also for the Evanston High School football home games. This report was very upsetting for the mayor and the council, and Mayor South made a point to tell the chief just that.

At that time the fire department was handling the ambulance services. Some of the volunteer firemen were certified as Emergency Medical Technicians (EMTs) and took care of all ambulance calls. This also upset a lot of citizens to think that anyone could be against this type of use from our voluntary fire/ambulance service. The mayor and council gave Cazin permission and their support to continue this commendable service. Cazin then asked about the ordinance to amend the revisions of the fire code.

At that time Ordinance 78-23 was introduced by me, amending and repealing sections in the revised code of the City of Evanston, relating to the fire prevention code. Title was read by City Attorney Lancaster, the motion was by Councilman Fruits to pass on first reading, seconded by Albrecht, with all voting in favor. Ordinance 78-23 was published in full by the Uinta County Herald and was passed on the second and third hearings with all voting in favor.

A public hearing was held to consider an appeal from Roger Fife on a conditional use permit. The Planning and Zoning Commission denied Fife the permit and now he was appealing to the council to overrule the decision. After some discussion the hearing was closed, and Councilman Fruits made a motion that the decision of the P & Z Commission be overruled and that Fife be granted a conditional use permit. The motion was seconded by Albrecht, with all voting in favor.

During this year all liquor licenses came up for renewal at the same time, because of a ruling made in 1977 by the council, at the liquor dealers request, to have all liquor licenses come up for renewal on the first regular meeting in October of each year prior to October 15th. Each request for renewal of the dealer's license was heard separately and acted upon separately. With no complaints filed by the police department on any of them, the licenses were all approved by regular motion and passed for renewal with all council members voting in favor.

Next on the agenda was a resolution annexing more property outside the city limits, introduced by me. The motion for adoption was made by Fruits, and seconded by Albrecht, with all voting in favor.

Mr. Jeff Carlson, Surveyor, presented a final plat of the Riverside Development Company, and was advised that the approval of the plat would have to be adopted by ordinance.

Other business taken care of at this meeting was the opening of two bids on two police vehicles, presented and accepted by motion. Steve Snyder of LUAG made his report on HUD grants, and a number of ordinances concerning parking, subdivisions, zoning, dedicating streets were all brought on the floor for their various readings, first, second and third, with proper motions made and seconded with all voting in favor. Finally the mayor reminded everyone about the special hearing concerning zoning on October 18th at 7:00 p.m. at the new city hall.

On October 18th Mayor Dan South opened the special hearing and explained that the purpose of it was to discuss the necessity of amending some ordinances that pertained to zoning and subdivisions. The hearing was called at the request of the Evanston Planning and Zoning Commission. Also, some changes in our ordinances concerning annexations and construction were talked about.

During the hearing the council took action to amend several ordinances that were recommended by P & Z and the council. Each amended ordinance was introduced and moved for approval on first reading with all voting in favor. All of the amended ordinances went on to be voted on second and third readings during the next few meetings with all voting in favor.

Also addressed at that meeting was the city engineer's recommendation for the sanitary sewer and the storm sewer to serve Uinta Downs properties, and a motion by Councilman Bills to pay the engineering fee for Oak Street as soon as it became a dedicated city street, seconded by Albrecht with all voting in favor.

Prior to adjourning, Mayor South told the group of citizens at the hearing that the city would like some recommendations from the public on what should be done with the old town hall building, which was built in 1915. The meeting and hearing adjourned at 10:30 p.m.

New traffic lights were installed by the Wyoming Highway Department at the intersection of 9th Street and Front Street, and the intersection of Main Street and Harrison Drive (11th Street). Although reports were that the traffic was moving smoothly, there seemed to be some confusion for drivers concerning right turns, especially at the intersection of 9th and Front near the underpass.

Highway Department personnel reported that Wyoming laws permit a right turn on a red light only after a stop and when no through traffic is moving. It didn't take long for the traffic to figure that out, but these traffic light locations were new to Evanston and it was a case of just getting used to them.

The General Election was held on November 7th with Governor Herschler winning again for a second term. In other elections, Mayor Dan South and S. Clark Anderson were voted in for county commissioners.

In the city election I was voted in as mayor by receiving 1232 votes against Keith Grover's 429 votes. In Ward 1, Russell A. Megeath defeated Vernon E. Smith. The vote was 308 to 244 in favor of Megeath; Ward 2 was won by incumbent Roy Fruits, who was unopposed. He received 347 votes; and Ward 3 was won by incumbent Ronald Davis defeating Margaret V. Smith, with 478 to 196 votes in favor of Davis.

I, as the newly elected mayor, and the new elected councilmen would assume office in January. Holdover council members were Russell Albrecht, Ward 1; James Rice, Ward 2; and David Bills, Ward 3.

After congratulations by everyone on their win in the election, Mayor South opened the regular city council meeting of November on Wednesday the 8th with the Pledge to the Flag and the approval of the previous minutes.

After a motion by Councilman Fruits, seconded by Davis to pay all outstanding bills, with all voting in favor, Roger Fife presented a bill for the easement and land for a storage tank on Red Mountain. I made a motion that the Joint Powers Board make payment for this bill as it was a debt connected to the water project. Fruits seconded the motion with all voting in favor.

A Mr. James Smith, representing a company in Provo, Utah made a presentation for conservation and water meters. The council expressed an interest but did not think the city was in need of these services at this time.

The council acted on several ordinances that had been pending, and there was a request for the city to participate in paying for the difference of the size of a proposed sewer line to Red Mountain Mesa Properties. The difference in size would be a 10-inch line rather than a 6-inch line.

This property was a subdivision owned by South and Jones Timber Company. Therefore Mayor South, part owner, excused himself from any discussion and from any vote by leaving the room because he felt that he had a conflict of interest in the request.

Councilman Albrecht then stated that it would be to the city's favor to have the larger line, therefore Albrecht made the motion that the sewer line be a 10-inch line and that the city make an effort to help pay for the difference in price. The motion was seconded by Bills, with all voting in favor. Before adjourning, I made a motion for the city to pay the difference of $10,000 to the Joint Powers Board to help pay off the water project from Revenue Sharing Funds. The motion was seconded by Fruits, all voting in favor. Adjournment was at 11:30 p.m.

The new two-lane bridge on Holland Drive over Bear River was installed and completed in November with a ribbon-cutting ceremony and Wilford Price, a long-time resident of North Evanston, being the first to cross the bridge. Mr. Price had seen the succession of bridges from a swinging footbridge to today's modern structure, plus he was one of the officials who placed the old one-way bridge that was installed in 1935. Also, at that time, Dr. Holland was Mayor of Evanston, and the decision was made to name the street Holland Drive.

The regular meeting of the Evanston City Council was held on December 6th. This would be the last and final meeting of the year. Mayor South had called in to be excused and I had called to tell the council that I was snowed in at Lyman and the roads were closed. Therefore, Mayor South and I both would be absent from this meeting.

Councilman Bills made a motion to appoint Councilman Davis, who held seniority, to be temporary Chairman to conduct the meeting, which was seconded by Albrecht with all voting in favor. Davis opened the meeting with the pledge to the flag.

Minutes of the past two meetings were read, corrected and approved by regular motion with all voting in favor, with a motion and second to approve all outstanding bills following, and all voting in favor.

During this meeting several outstanding ordinances concerning zoning, subdivisions, and annexations were acted upon for second and third readings. There was a short discussion on each ordinance before motions and seconds were made, with all voting in favor. Also a resolution was introduced and acted upon to authorize the city to sell the old Holland Drive Bridge to Richard Sims. Mr. Sims's bid of $750 was the only one received. Councilman Albrecht made the motion to adopt the resolution, seconded by Rice with all voting in favor.

After the adoption of a few other resolutions, other business that was acted on was the discussion of the golf course and its condition, what to do with the Old Town Hall building, and repairs to the old garbage truck and a motion by Councilman Fruits to pay all full time employees a year-end Christmas bonus of $25.00 each, seconded by Rice, with all voting in favor.

1978 was almost over and Mayor Dan South was on his way out as mayor. In January 1979 he would be sworn in as one of the new county commissioners.

I congratulated Dan on his successful term as mayor, and I mean successful. He had a pretty tough four years with problems of growth and the Vehar bombing in August of 1977. I believe he handled everything very well, considering. Every year he worked with a balanced budget, and it wasn't easy because of the problems being caused by fast growth. This had a huge effect on the funds not coming in fast enough to keep up with the problems. He kept an adequate and capable group of city employees without having to make any cuts. Dan was a very public-minded person and in my opinion he would make a good County Commissioner, and I also congratulated him on his successful win as commissioner

ACKNOWLEDGMENTS

This book would never have been written if it hadn't been for a number of people who had assisted me in remembering some of the events and occurrences mentioned in the book, and making minutes of meetings and other materials available to me. In showing my appreciation I wish to name those folks.

First of all, I would like to thank my wife Sandy for all her support and encouragement she gave me to help me through this book. There were many times when I was ready to quit, but with her encouragement and her editing, I was able to get it finished.

I also wish to thank Maryl Thompson, Receptionist and Administrative Assistant of my real estate agency, Uinta Realty, Inc., for all the assistance she gave me in using my computer. When I had a computer problem, she was always on hand to help me through it, as did Tonya Dennis, Associate Broker in the office, who also assisted me on the computer when necessary.

Also, I want to thank the Executive Assistant to the Mayor of Evanston and Deputy City Clerk Nancy Stevenson for her time and hard work in providing me with 16 years of copies of the minutes of all the official meetings of the Evanston City Council during my tenure as Mayor of Evanston, 1979-1983 and 1987-1995, plus the term of Mayor Gene Martin, 1983-1987.

Other folks I wish to thank and show appreciation to are Shelly and Deann Horne of Creative Ink Images for their assistance in preparing the book cover; and Former City Engineer Brian Honey for information he provided me concerning the Sulphur Creek Dam Project and many other projects that were constructed during my term as Mayor. Brian was City Engineer under me for my last eight years in office. Thanks are also due to City Attorney Dennis Boal for straightening me out on a few matters. Dennis was my City Attorney also during my final eight years of my term as mayor. Thanks also to retired Urban Renewal Agency Director Jim Davis for providing me with information for my book; and former City Councilmember Tom Hutchinson for the information and input that he provided me. Other city employees that I wish to thank are Paul Knopf, former city planner, Public Works Superintendent Allan "Oop" Hansen and Engineering Tech Bob Liechty for their input to my story.

I also want to thank the Uinta County Library in Evanston for the use of their equipment, the Uinta County Museum in Evanston and the Evanston Chamber of Commerce for materials provided me to be used in my book; and the Uinta County Herald for giving me the opportunity to look through many of their old newspapers.

I appreciate all those named above for the completion of this book Evanston, Wyoming…Boom-Bust-Politics.

However, I want to let you, the reader, know that almost all of the material used in this story was from my personal collection of photos, newspaper clippings, letters, etc., and from the actual minutes of the Evanston meetings during the period from 1967 to 1995. But some material is also from my own memory and from talking to some of those folks I mentioned above.

Thank You…

April 25, 2018

ABOUT THE AUTHOR

Born January 28, 1932 in Salt Lake City, Utah, Dennis ended up in Evanston, Wyoming. He quit high school and joined the 141st Tank Battalion of the Wyoming National Guard.

When the Korean War started in 1950, his unit was called to active duty in September, but he and his wife, Sandy got married on July 26, 1950 before he left for active duty, and to serve time in Korea.

Dennis and Sandy settled in Evanston, where he served three 4-year terms as a member of the Evanston city council and three 4-year terms as mayor. Dennis retired at the age of 81 from his real estate agency, and after raising four sons and over 68 years of marriage, he and his wife Sandy still reside in Evanston.

> **Be sure to look for**
> **Volume 2 of Evanston Wyoming**

CPSIA information can be obtained
at www.ICGtesting.com
Printed in the USA
BVHW032130180119
538202BV00003B/4/P